MARILYN ACROSS AMERICA

The Continental Divide Ride

Jeff Fletcher

For

Chuck and Patti Powers

And

Samantha

The information provided in this book is for the purpose of entertainment. It is meant to give as complete an example as possible. The reader no matter how experienced with motorcycles or off-road riding should exercise extreme care and caution in all circumstances. Motorcycles and riding can be dangerous, and we are not liable for any injuries, death, or damage due to the inherent risk involved with motorcycle riding activities.

Marilyn Gets Around

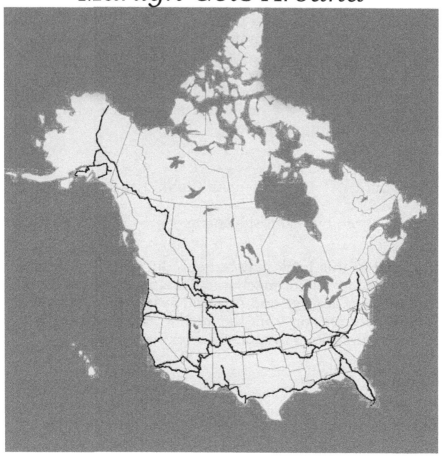

Table of Contents

PROLOGUE   11

LONELY ROADS AND LOVELY LADIES   19

DECISIONS TO BE MADE...   35

ON THE ROAD TO CANADA, HOW DID I ARRIVE AT
WORLD WAR II?   43

PAVEMENT DAY IDAHO HWY 26   55

DAY 1   63

DAY 2   73

DAY 3   89

DAY 4   105

DAY 5   123

DAY 6   149

DAY 7   175

DAY 9   199

DAY 10   211

DAY 11   223

DAY 12   229

DAY 13 AND 14   237

DAY 15   255

DAY 16 AND 17   261

DAY 18   275

DAY 19   283

EPILOGUE   291

CREDITS AND SOURCES   295

RECOMMENDATIONS   298

Prologue

The year is 2015.

I am camped in Ridgway, Colorado. It's late in the Summer, nearly Fall. I think it's a Friday but am unsure. I've been here a month, slowly working my way towards a plan.

By 7pm, the plan is complete.

Somewhere around midnight the whole thing exploded.

Before the stroke of twelve I had planned to take a leisurely ride on two wheels, following the Continental Divide. Enjoying the scenery. Keeping it simple.

Then, at midnight I saw him. And her.

I knew them both. One I had left behind. The other I was just getting to know.

For days now, the Continental Divide has consumed my thoughts, and my reading. And soon, my sleep.

I had drawn a blue line on a map along the high ridges of the mountain ranges between northern Montana and southern New Mexico.

I want to ride that blue line.

Until midnight it was just a line, then, it became personal. It also transformed from blue to red. The color of conflict.

Water on one side flows west, on the other side, east. Water that has provided growth for tall trees, irrigation for agriculture, filled creeks, rivers and high mountain lakes; grown grasses and edibles for wildlife, in general fuelling the lives of those who have called the area home for hundreds, if not thousands of years.

I came to Ridgway to visit a friend and to make day rides on two wheels, along the old mining roads surrounding Ridgway, Telluride and Ouray.

I ride these historic haul roads on a Suzuki DR650. It isn't new and fresh and it isn't old and breaking down. Neither am I, new nor breaking down.

One day sitting in a coffee shop in Ouray, I read of the Continental Divide Ride. Spur of the moment, I decide to make the ride.

Evenings, since the decision, have been spent reading history and loading GPS tracks.

This evening, reading complete, I finish off the remaining quarter ounce of Scotch, swirled in a glass of crushed ice, and left to sit until the twelve-year-old blend becomes cold and fine.

I turn off the campers 12-volt light, and slip away into nature's own cocktail, nitrogen and oxygen, the mix having less oxygen here, elevated high in these San Juan mountains.

Sleep comes.

Then I see him.

A lone rider atop a horse. Framed against the western sky.

The horse stands on a small knoll near what is today the border of Montana and Idaho. The riders posture reflects both pride and defeat. He is aware of a certain truth, but he will not abide it.

He looks down at the woman standing to his side, her eyes upward and hopeful.

"I met you on a horse. I came to know you on a horse. It is fitting that I will return to you on a horse."

"There must be someplace we can go." She pleads.

"We have nowhere left to go."

He adds. "So, we will fight."

She knows he is right, knows she cannot stop him, doesn't want to stop him. Still, she hears herself say.

"Maybe if we talk to them again." She is almost in tears.

He gently interrupts, "There has been talk. But there is not enough land. And now, the land and the talk have met."

His eyes move from the infinite western sky downward to hers. Seeing her emotion, his manner changes from violent resolve to a kindness cultivated and understood between the two of them. An understanding they have shared for many years.

"This horse is strong. But I fear he is not strong enough. My father met them many times. I stood and watched as he welcomed the first ones. We should have killed them then and there."

He raises one arm high, defiant, holds it there, then turns and rides away leaving her alone with her fears.

With a start, I awake. I see her face. *I know her.*

The clock reads 12:15. I shake my head. I am not one to remember dreams. They may come and they may go, but they go without leaving a trace of memory.

This dream is different. There was color, texture and voice. Texture and color as real as the burgundy and tan blanket under which I lie. I rotate the pillow for a fresh beginning. At that point I realize.

It comes to me like one of those moments searching for a name that will not appear until we stop searching. Of course. Has to be. I've spent several days reading about the history of western Montana. Conflict between a certain Western Tribe and settlers who grew in numbers, year by year.

All of that history came together to interrupt my sleep.

Early history explains the man on the horse. Recent history explains the woman.

In eight hours', time, I awake, suit up and ride the Suzuki ten minutes down the road to a coffee shop.

My name is Jeff Fletcher. I am a musician. I used to be other things. Things left behind. Things that served a purpose at the time, now mostly a memory, discarded like an old suit and tie, the circumstances for their need no longer on the front page of my life. It's the back pages I now peruse. Leaving the headlines to others.

This is the story of a back page motorcycle ride. Headlines are written on the super slab expressways. This ride will make use of the tiny lines on a topography map.

The ride is called the Great Continental Divide Ride. It runs north to south. It begins in the territory of the Nez Perce, the tribe of my dream. It ends at the border of the United States and Mexico. Covering approximately two thousand miles of dirt roads, most of them at an altitude best suited to snow skis and wild animals and chilly temperatures.

Anyone can make this ride. GPS routes are widely available. All it takes is time. Time and two wheels. Or two legs as I will later discover.

A few, following in the history of the Nez Perce have made the journey on horseback. I prefer two wheels. Be it ten horsepower or a thousand, or human powered, the result is the same. Time well spent.

This book is about time well spent. It is also about history, motorcycles, danger, breakdowns, women, men, romance and yes, dirt roads. Dirt roads and pathways, some of them wrinkled with age, others, mere toddlers.

The dust permeates, then and still does today, the lives and visions of the men and women who lived and breathed that dust. Roads that transported their lives into commerce, into peril, into cultural upheaval and for the most part, simply took them back home.

When roads roll beneath the wheels of a motorcycle, there is time to reflect. Echoes from ones past have a way of bouncing back. Through the trees along the road. Off the mountains. Even reflecting from the waters of creeks, rivers and lakes passed along the way.

The past, it is said, weighs heavy with the passage of time. A weight which can be a burden or a delight, depending on the mood of the day.

The best roads, like a good song have a beginning, a middle and an end. They often have a message, though it isn't to be found in words or in a four-count beat or in melody. The roads communicate in a more elusive manner.

Some tell you to slow down, winding curve upon curve, following alongside a remote river as it flows over the oldest and hardest of rock. Others entice you to charge full steam ahead, flying towards a faint horizon with golden meadows on each side, narrowing ones focus to the road ahead.

Still others give up their message gently, one tenth of a mile at a time, changing in temperature, altitude, cloud state, light, sounds, road surface condition and your own disposition.

The people met along the way also tell a story, some reluctantly.

Are they curious about a helmeted, dusty rider who appears into their world, if only for a moment? Do they share a conversation, revealing a tiny portion of themselves? Do they lower their eyes and walk sternly ahead, out of disinterest or fear or simply out of time?

My ride will run north to south, although the compass has little to do with the direction one travels along this route. The true bearing is an inner track, never remotely aware the direction towards which the front wheel turns.

A month or two before debarking on this ride, I was scanning the internet for music (my set list needed some fresh songs). As I listened to song after song, I happened upon a video of a man singing a tune that I would never attempt, never add to my own set list. But still, I listened. I listened until the very end.

Sung by Andrea Bocelli, the song was "Con Te Partiro", meaning "I will leave with you". The lyrics, and the man, speak of the many contradictions of life. Gifts given and those ungranted. A final note held with the purity of God's own conscience.

Translation of the lyrics reveals a story of romantic notions existing side by side with reflective sadness.

Bocelli takes the stage and sings of lost love and of seas that no longer exist.

Like Con Te Partido's lyrics, hidden beneath today's Continental Divide roads, there are paths that no longer exist. Some paved over with small towns. Others buried below new gravel, along with four-hundred-year-old foot prints, lost to time.

But they are there.

If I stop periodically along the blue line, looking closely, perhaps I will see them.

Hundreds of people have made this ride over paths that no longer exist.

If you are wondering if you should add your name to the list, I hope that somewhere in these pages, you find an answer.

Lonely Roads and Lovely Ladies

After my dream and the extra sleep, I enter a coffee shop in Ridgway.

I'm wearing a blue textile armored jacket, blue textile armored pants and a pair of well-worn motocross boots.

I walk to the queue and read the menu handwritten in white chalk on a black board behind the bar.

The barista is in her late thirties. She wears cutoff jeans and a short sleeve tie-dye T shirt. Around her neck is a bronze kokopelli suspended from a leather loop. Her fingers hold five rings of various shapes and sizes. Three on the left hand, two on the right. A simple gold band circles her right thumb. I am not educated in current matrimonial symbols. I want to ask about the gold band, but do not.

Her hair is long and blonde, pulled back and braided. She has the confident manner of good breeding and good looks. Her wardrobe slightly aimed below her age, yet she pulls it off. Rather well, I thought.

She smiles, noticing my blue attire. Looking me up and down, she hesitates, then can't help herself.

"I've never gotten to serve a Smurf before." She almost giggled, showing dimples and panache.

"It's just a pigment of your imagination." Says I.

"How many times have you used that line?"

"A few, but never to one as lovely." I was shameless. But honest. I gave her a cautious smile. One usually reserved for government officials.

"Aww, aren't you sweet. But the coffee is still three fifty, and the muffin is three twenty-five. Ridgway may be less expensive than ritzy Telluride, just down the road, but not by much.

You can't win em all, I thought to myself.

My heart wasn't in it anyway. It had been stolen a few months earlier in New River, Arizona. The lady in question was not aware. I was aware but knew she was unobtainable. And I was ok with that. Sort of. At any rate, I could live with it.

She could live in my dreams.

Still, inwardly smiling at panache and low-cut tie die, I sit my overly blue attire back into a comfy chair and briefly wondered if blue clashed with brown leather. Deciding that the self-awareness of age and the relaxation of retirement could handle blue on brown, I plucked the top off the muffin, and wolfed it down. Dang, that's good. Maybe even worth the price.

A map of the entire United States is folded inside my jacket pocket. I take it out. I'm only interested in a part of it. The scale of this map does not show the roads I seek, but I know they are there. The lonely roads.

The high mountain roads that are not there have long been associated with challenge, hardship, severity and discomfort. I could use a small dose of that discomfort, if camping each night at the Holiday Inn qualifies. Early explorers of this western line slept under the light of the moon. I'll sleep under a neon sign, content with day time exploration.

I have grown easy. Languid and listless. Memories of adventure have faded. Personal challenge has also faded. Complacency has crept across my landscape like a fog. I need a warm clearing wind, and I knew just where to find it.

I know because of the writings of a man named Mark Sampson. Two years earlier, Mark had unknowingly led me towards another long motorcycle ride, called the Trans-America Trail, a collection of dirt roads leading East to West, spanning five thousand, five hundred miles from Tennessee to the coast of Oregon.

Taken as a whole, the ride seemed undoable. Taken one day at a time, I was able to see it through.

Once more, Mark, unknowingly leads me towards some dirt. This time on the road to the Continental Divide.

(Side note. Years later, I would have the pleasure of riding with Mark in Patagonia, Arizona and the pleasure of meeting his lovely wife, Debbi. A finer couple you will never meet.)

Back to the lonely roads......

To attempt once again to see it through. An inner wind is brewing. It propels me out of the camper and into the wilds, such as they are in days when wild isn't the same wild as a few hundred years past. I need a long ride.

The Great Continental Divide Ride.

The internet in this coffee shop reveals the recent history of this route. A hearty few blazed the first trail. We all follow in the literal or figurative footsteps of others.

So, I ask myself who was first to traverse from Canada to Mexico?

Turns out, it all began with a poem, a tenacious man and a desire which would not be denied. Someone had to be first. The first to say, "I think I'll walk from Canada to Mexico."

The likely original, took the first steps in southern Arizona over a century ago.

Peter Parsons, a thirty-five-year-old Swedish Immigrant, hiked south to north, from the border of Mexico to the border of Canada. There were no well-traveled trails. There wasn't much of a map. Piecing together mining trails, railroad tracks, two lane roads, prospector paths, game trails and river bottoms, he stubbornly worked his way north.

Barney Scout Mann, who has done considerable research on Peter Parsons, believes he carried compass, rifle, hand ax, pistol, ammunition, frying pan, canteen, sleeping bag, a folding camera and a grub bag (consisting of rice, beans, raisons and bacon and flour). Likely sixty pounds of gear.

Parsons left behind over a thousand pages of his journal and seven hundred photo negatives. With such a trove of writing and photos, perhaps there is an answer to what drove Peter Parsons to embark on such a journey?

Mr. Mann, surmises that Parsons had been inspired by the poems of Robert Service. Parsons had copied sections of "The Spell of the Yukon" into his journal. Parsons had visited Alaska and was moved by its immense unbearable wildness. He kept the words of Robert Service in his journal.

The strong life that never knows harness,

The wilds where the caribou call,

The freshness, the freedom, the farness,

O God, how I am stuck on it all.

Little did he know that the footprints he left behind, along a trek of approximately two thousand miles would serve as inspiration for generations of others to abandon comfort, hearth and home to embark on their own strong life.

Over the next hundred years, more trails would be blazed, maps drawn, paths worn and finally names given to each section of what would become the Continental Divide thru hike route. It is not known how much of today's route follows Parsons's path. Nor does it matter. Your own route will follow your own path, as Parsons did his.

What is today's Continental Divide route will surely not be the same route in fifty years. Things change. They always do.

As bicycles became more adept at off road ease, and people being people, soon there was a route for off road bicycles. Some of the route overlapping the hiker's route, some unique.

Not to be left out, off road motorcyclist, added their own tracks. Again, some of the route overlaps the hikers and bicyclist route, some is unique to motorcycles. One thing leads to another. One perception transforms into something new. Or mostly new. Borrowing from those who go before, taking a little of this, a little of that. Adding a side trail here, a detour there. Soon enough time and invention come together to allow modern day Peter Parsons to download a GPS track and follow it like cookie crumbs. Only it's not the same. Not even close.

Still, perception and habit and contemporary life experience do not prepare one to travel such roads. Perception must be adjusted. Habits changed. Life experiences of a gas station and fast food and a mechanic on every exit and every other corner must be forgotten.

Self-reliance and preparation and a little bit of luck become the golden keys to unlock a golden ride.

Today, few who ride motorcycles along this route will carry a compass. Fewer still pack flour and bacon. Some will make daily entries into a journal. Some have read the words of Robert Service. Times, they may be a changing, but inspiration does not require a satellite navigation system.

As America has grown and science has grown with it, the roads of America have changed. Horse and buggy paths and the two-lane country jaunts of old do not serve the needs of a population living mostly within city limits.

Miles and miles of long and lovely dirt roads still crisscross the land, following rivers and valleys, some semi smooth like pebbled glass, others offering up an experience akin to an ant, careening over forty grit sandpaper lying on the upward slope on a child's playground slide. These roads still exist. They just aren't the norm in most people's lives.

Most of us are more familiar with maps showing interstate highways that are four and six and even eight and ten lanes wide. The highways, like those who travel them are busy, full, ever moving, built with the need to arrive. A destination. Not a journey. The concrete and asphalt are symbols of efficiency. Long ago bypassing places and towns whose location was no longer the fastest way to here or to there. The highways hum with competence and commerce.

There are, however, more miles of blessed isolation in this country than highways. For a few two wheeled travelers, their voice and their secrets beckon like a mermaid on a distant shore.

These are the roads of the Continental Divide Ride.

The route changes year to year. Sometimes because the Forest Service abandons old roads, other times because property changes hands, gates are locked, or severe washouts require a reroute. Care need be taken when downloading a GPS route that is several years old. Such an outdated plan may steer you smack into a dead end of sorts, requiring a long back track, where hopefully your fuel on board will allow such a back track.

Ridden in its entirety one's odometer, because of the meandering nature of the route, will show approximately two thousand two hundred miles of travel. Five states will pass beneath your wheels. States which did not exist when many of these paths were first walked. Game and hunters' paths, which later became dirt roads ran through what was known as The Oregon Territory, The Mexican Cession and The Unorganized Territory.

Prior to Europe's movement west, prior to Christopher Columbus, before there was such a nomenclature as The Oregon Territory, people lived in North America and they themselves wandered and made lives along the high paths and through the green valley's making up what we today call the Rocky Mountains.

Those people surely could never have imagined a petrol powered, dual sport motorcycle. Nor would they have reason to foresee a future of paved trails connecting one village to another. Yet, they walked and later rode on horseback along the very rivers and through the same high passes through which I was planning to steer a motorcycle.

Parsons was escaping poor prospects in his homeland. Robert Service came from some of Scotland's finest schools. Despite disparate backgrounds both were transformed by wilderness.

Before Parsons, those who called the wilderness of western North America home are known by names such as Teton Sioux, Nez Perce, Blackfeet, Salish, Shoshone and many others.

Long before Europeans walked the high trails along the Continental Divide those tribes told a story bound to and inspired by the land as surely as those who came later. Their future as unknown to them as the grass hidden beneath a harsh winter's snowfall.

As I sit sipping coffee and reflect on that history and its effect upon my proposed ride, I realize that the future of my ride is also unknown.

My coffee is still warm. The Colorado summer air flows through the open window.

Into this air flows the unseen waves of a wireless internet. I use these unseen waves to learn more about the lives of those who came before Robert Service and Peter Parsons who roamed the remote pathways of the Continental Divide.

The year was 15,000 BC...

Peoples of the Asian Continent, for reasons largely unknown, but likely due to natural disasters, war or following herds of animals, crossed what was then a frozen sea in the Bearing Strait.

Through the centuries, tribes developed. Some prospered, others floundered. Land was fought and died for.

We tend to underestimate those who came before. Yet, in many ways we remain the same.

As populations grew, inhabitants became an influence on the land, the animals, the lakes and the trails. Like an oasis in the desert, some land has better weather, more water, larger herds of game. This is the land which tribes fought to control, driving out those already there and then fighting to retain it. European settlers do not hold a monopoly on such behavior.

Some of these earliest inhabitants worked their way southward from British Columbia into the northwestern section of today's United States. They walked the high-altitude Continental Divide, hunting, foraging; in general, making a life.

While contemplating ancient history, I sit in a relatively young town. Ridgway. It is a typical and completely untypical small town in the Rocky Mountains. Typical in its high-altitude Colorado beauty, drawing transplants from around the country and indeed from around the world. Just down the road about thirty miles, tucked into a sheer walled canyon is the fashionable ski town, Telluride.

Today, in chic and crowded Telluride, a vacation is likely to involve a small amount of traffic. I'm not fanatical about traffic, I'm just slightly jealous that I don't own one of those Telluride condos, slope side.

Here in Ridgway, there is different sort of chic. Larger land plots. Smaller crowds. Less celebrity. There is even talk of paving the town roads. An improvement perhaps. Telluride was mostly paved, years ago.

Ridgway has had its share of famous visitors and has its share of famous residents. Ralph Lauren of polo playing shirt emblem fame has a substantial working ranch on the outskirts of town.

John Wayne paid a visit to film the iconic "True Grit". A few of the buildings used in the movie still stand. Visitors shouldn't miss the opportunity to dine at "The Grit" on the main street, where the view from an upstairs balcony overlooks the bucolic park lined with historic buildings.

A sliver of light falls along my map, forming an illumination running exactly north to south. Canada to Mexico. Hmmm. That pretty much sums it up. Maybe it's a sign. Maybe it's just sun light. Maybe I need another cup of coffee.

There is a casualness to this coffee shop and to its patrons. Ridgway is mostly a tourist destination and a second home community. Few of the patrons seem rushed. Few wears facial stress lines alluding to clients who need appeasing or overdue bills that can no longer be ignored. My own stress is dialed back. It's been in such a state for some time now. The path to such a mindset could fill a book. In fact, it has.

"Marilyn Across America" Book 1, The Trans-America Trail, was a personal attempt to understand past decisions and past consequence. It's available on Amazon if you are curious. It details a fifty-five-hundred-mile cross country motorcycle journey through dust, dirt, heartache and joy.

Today, joining the other casual patrons my stress factors and my needs are few. Life choices, like coffee and creamer, are a balance. Needs on one side. Wants on the other. Needs have a way of forcing the issue. Wants can be curtailed, cajoled, rationalized and dismissed. If the sunlight were to rise from the map to my face, few lines of discourse would show.

Sipping coffee and wiping muffin crumbs from my chin, I see, outside the window, not John Wayne, nor his trusty steed, but my own carriage.

It doesn't trot. It doesn't gallop. Instead, it rolls along on one of man's grandest inventions. The wheel.

If the average motorcycle rider were to spot this white, blue and black beauty outside this coffee shop, they might label it a dual sport motorcycle. Others call it an enduro, slang for the days of endurance events on large off-road motorcycles. Call it dual sport. Call it an enduro, or just call it a motorcycle.

I call it Marilyn.

Marilyn isn't bred for speed. She does not resemble muscle carved from marble. Her pedigree is not traced to Secretariat or Man O War. I don't need speed. I need a rugged nature. I need a mule.

My mule is held together by nuts and by bolts and by the geometry of triangular frames, welded and wrestled into place on an assembly line far away by workers with last names I would stumble trying to pronounce.

It is simple in design and simply elegant in purpose. Two rubber tires sprout pronounced knobs at odd angles, ready to produce tractor-like friction over the small patch of earth on which they roll.

A white five-gallon gas tank holds enough dinosaur bones to claw and paw and careen over two hundred miles of that earth before a pause to refill.

In a hundred years, the dinosaur bones will likely be replaced by lithium, if indeed the earth has enough. Lithium that is.

For now, a single 12-volt battery turns a starter motor and fires the beast to life. A blue seat with red piping holds its pilot into place in a semblance of comfort and provides a hint of style.

Soft textile black luggage slung over the rear sub frame is the modern-day replacement for leather saddlebags. Lacking in nostalgia, but also without the need of stables, grain, hay, iron shoes and a shovel to clean up the organic nature of the beast.

Take your pick, horse and cow flatulence or a muffler. Ain't never a free lunch.

But this book isn't about such decisions. Hindsight is purity of vision, like stones, to swords, to bow and arrow to flint lock, two feet to four legs, turning wheels becomes computer science and unseen waves of Wi-Fi.

Next step? We insert probes into our frontal cortex to merely think of moving icons across a screen and it is done. Beam me up Scotty.

Hopefully along the way to all of this "progress" the lonely roads still call.

Together my mule and I have not won a single race, but we have ridden to some pretty cool places.

Two years ago, we left tire and boot prints in the Oregon sand. Now, I'd like to leave a few tracks at the border of Mexico.

As I sit in this Colorado coffee shop, day dreaming of turning wheels and tie dye, I see the motorcycle again through the window.

On each side of the gas tank is a decal of the one and only Marilyn. That singular image always draws smiles at gas stations. I'd met many a character because of the image of a woman long ago gone but forever remembered. Why a decal of a blonde bombshell on a motorcycle? Because even a mule aspires to a higher calling.

It might not be possible to put lipstick on a pig, but Marilyn on a mule works out just fine.

I focus once again on the blue line.

If the men and women of America's Western history could walk and or ride horseback along those high mountain passes, surely, I could manage the task on a motorcycle with a modern suspension.

They also had to build their own homes and its furniture. If they wanted to eat, they either grew it or killed it. Perspective is sometimes encouraging.

The incredulity of sitting in a leather chair that I did not build, drinking coffee I did not have to brew, munching on a muffin I did not have to bake while using technology to read of the exploits of those who roamed the Western Continental Divide was not lost on me.

The muffin slowly disappears leaving crumbs for a future mouse to trace back to this comfy chair.

The coffee needs a refill. My blue attire should present itself once more to a barista whom, I'm sure could use another reason to grin.

I approach the coffee bar.

"Are you still here?" She raises one eyebrow as she asks.

I think she actually blushed. Or maybe it was warm back there with all that coffee.

"My tribe doesn't leave until noon. We always travel in packs." It was the best line I could come up with on short notice.

"There is no way, more than one person has that same outfit."

Touché.

"You cut me deep Shrek. You cut me deep." Says I.

She actually guffawed. Complete with a slight snort. I was quite proud.

"I haven't heard that line in years. I looooove Shrek."

"Eddy boddy love Shrek. Like Eddy boddy love parfait. And eddy boddy love muffins." Says I. What the heck, in for a Shrek penny, in for a Shrek pound.

"You are funny." Says tie die. "But we don't have parfait."

"OK, then, how about another muffin and one more cup of mild coffee?"

"I have one left. Never thought it would sell. It may be left over from yesterday. How about half price?"

"I'll take it." My Ridgway economy was improving.

Back to the chair. The coffee was fine. The muffin was stale. But a fair wind was blowing.

My enthusiasm was roaring through this coffee shop, across the old bricks of "The Grit", through the trees and the Aspen lined clearing where The Duke, played a steady but flawed Marshall named Rooster Cogburn.

Cogburn once sat astride a chestnut quarter horse and eyed the bad guys across the field, poised on their own steeds, ready to line their trail with more death.

Marshall Cogburn knew the odds as four to one. He knew he was out gunned. He could have retreated to regroup. He could have picked another fight on another day, with odds more in his favor. He did neither. Instead, before taking the reins in his teeth and charging full gallop into the fray, he exclaimed "Fill your hand you Son of a Bitch".

I wondered what The Duke would think of riding a motorcycle instead of a horse through these aspen lined meadows. There may be no buckshot or lead rushing past one's helmeted head, nonetheless, a "fill your hand you S.O.B. attitude won't hurt.

Hmmm. I can do this. Maybe a couple weeks of easy paced riding. Might be fun. Might temporarily cure my laziness.

Coffee, I did not brew. Internet I cannot fully explain. I grin inwardly, laughing into the rising steam, pondering the love life of a smurf.

Decisions to be Made...

How much chrome does one guy need?

Before ordering coffee from beautiful baristas, one must actually ride to Ridgway. Before making that ride, one must choose a motorcycle.

Women are said to love Harleys but if you want to ride dirt, it won't be on chrome. Women will have to be impressed by your charm, not your chrome, which leaves me in big trouble.

When planning any long ride on two wheels, there are decisions to be made. What shall I wear? Leather, textile, Gore-Tex, jeans? Should I camp or stay in hotels? What color helmet would be best? Full face helmet, half helmet, no helmet? How much food should I carry? How much water? How many tools?

Even though I've ridden my share of miles, both on road and off, I am not a motorcycle expert. I'm not a mechanic. I'm just another guy with an opinion.

So, here is my opinion. I chose textile. With built in crash armor. Waterproof. Merely because it's easier for me than donning rain gear. I chose a bright colored full-face helmet. All of the comely lasses met along the way don't give a hoot. But hopefully motorist see me coming.

I chose to carry a days' worth of water, in case I break down, can't repair the motorcycle and need to walk some distance. I chose to carry only a days' worth of food, because again, I may need to hike to a road, but in this country, one is rarely more than a long day hike from a paved road and safety. I chose hotels because, one, thankfully my budget allows it, and two, sleeping on the ground is not my favorite cup of tea. Sure, I also carry a waterproof bivy, just in case, but so far, I've never used it.

The experience of traveling dirt roads in remote places, for some, is enhanced by camping. More power to em. In years gone by, I would also have chosen to camp. Just not in these years.

I chose to carry enough tools to repair almost anything that can go wrong with my particular motorcycle. Tire repair tools, inner tube patch kit, tire irons, spare inner tube for front and rear tires. A wrench and Allen tool for every nut and Allen head on the bike. A chain repair tool. Two master links for that particular chain. A hand air pump and a small 12-volt battery operated pump.

For detailed, and I mean very detailed, ideas of what to bring on your own long ride, I highly recommend viewing several guys on the web. First, look up Mark Sampson, of Big Dog Adventures. He outlines his gear, his bikes, how he sets up his bikes, his riding gear and his tools. He has about a hundred thousand dirt road miles under his dual sport belt. He knows a thing or two.

I also recommend the writings of RTWPaul. Round The World Paul. He also goes into great detail about tools, tents, food, bike set up, and on and on. Paul could rebuild a dual sport motorcycle alongside of the road with a multi tool and duct tape. I once watched a video of him, towing another dual sport for about seventy miles. Sometimes ya gotta do what ya gotta do, but holy smoke, that is a level of patience that few possess. Paul also knows a thing or two.

For the faster riders out there, check out the videos of Lyndon Poskitt. He is an off-road racer who also has ridden much of the world. His videos also get into excellent detail about tools, camping gear and bike set up. Lydon, like Paul and Mark, carries the tools needed for his motorcycle. Not for the one you own. They might be the same tools. They might not.

Now, for the most asked question!!!!!!

Ready? You know what is coming don't you? You've heard it a thousand times, haven't you? It's been answered by at least a hundred off road riders, on a hundred forums.

What motorcycle should I take?????

Well, I have your answer. The one you already own. Unless, of course, you own a giant street bike. Then the answer to what bike to take is...... The one you can afford, understand how to repair and desire to own.

There is simply no best bike.

But we still think there is. Don't we?

Why? You know that answer also.

If you are a guy, it's because, as I have written before, analyzing is what guys do. We can't help ourselves. We create spread sheets. If we enjoy baseball, we look up batting averages, on base percentage, strike outs.

If we enjoy dual sports, we research miles per gallon. Horsepower per pound of weight. We judge this suspension better over that suspension, because, well because our favorite long-distance off-road rider uses that suspension so it must be better.

Ride the bike you already own and outfit it in a suitable manner, don't go overboard, just enough of this and not too much of that. You need some sort of luggage. You don't need the latest and greatest in LED lighting. You need a gas tank that will carry you about 180 miles between fill ups. You don't need a 12-gallon Baja Tank that you once saw an off road across Africa rider using.

One of my riding semi-heroes, Ted Simon, rode a 500 cc Triumph around the world. He began his ride in 1973. The Triumph wasn't perfect. It sometimes broke down. He repaired it. Or more likely, Ted being Ted, found someone who could. He never professed to be a mechanic. I can relate. His good humor made the day.

On his first trip, he was very modestly sponsored by a British newspaper known as The Sunday Times. In exchange for periodic articles, Mr. Simon had the means to keep going. And keep going he did. Forty-five countries and sixty-four thousand miles later, he victoriously rode back to England. He was forty-two years old when he began his long uncertain globe circling endeavor. He was forty-six when he finished. Compare this to a two-week ride along the high ridges of the Western United States and the humble almost silly nature of such a two-week ride becomes evident.

When Ted was seventy, for reasons he himself has admitted were a combination of circumstance and coincidence, he did it again. Ted decided to re-create his around the world trip. But, alas, he didn't own a suitable motorcycle. Ted, put the word out.

Next thing he knows, someone loaned him a suitable BMW for the trip. Mind you, he had to give it back after the trip, but still, now he had a bike. Ted's BMW wasn't the latest, the most powerful, with the best possible suspension. In fact, it was old, but rebuilt.

It was an R80GS.

It worked out just fine. Sure, things broke, in fact, at one point Ted himself broke. His leg. But he healed and rode on. He dealt with the issues as they arose. The choice of motorcycle had little to do with his success.

Ted's first book, "Jupiter's Travels", and his second book, "Dreaming of Jupiter", describe the countries through which he road, politics, romance, motorcycles, how the countries changed from his first trip to his second and Ted's own metamorphosis.

Anyone who rides long distances on a motorcycle will soon learn, it's never about the motorcycle. It's about you.

Read that last line again.

The motorcycle is a tool. The ride is the goal. The motorcycle isn't the goal. If it is the goal, then you might not really want to make that long ride. And that's ok. But if you do actually desire to make that long off-road ride, then make the ride with any bike you can get your hands on.

If you like to ride fast, buy a KTM. If you want comfort and don't mind by passing some of the more technical sections of a particular ride, get a big BMW GS, or one of the larger KTMs. If you want simple, affordable, buy a KLR 650, DR 650, DRZ 400, WR250R, CRF250 and others of that ilk.

Mark Sampson has owned more off road, dual sport motorcycles than most. He has ridden thousands of miles on all of them. So, why buy a different one every few years? I suspect because it's fun. He truly enjoys setting up the bikes to his liking. And he's very good at it.

But he will tell you it's not a requirement to make long journeys. Mark rode over fifty thousand off road miles on a Yamaha WR250R. His friend, and mine, Scott Stevenson, also put over fifty thousand miles on a 2009 WR250R. Sure, there are faster, better suspended, perhaps more comfortable dual sport bikes out there, and if you have the means, by all means, buy one.

Speaking of Scott Stevenson, do yourself a favor and visit 3 Step Hideaway in southeastern Utah, run by Scott and his wife Julie. I have no idea how many riders have visited their place over the years, but I do know that after visiting they all consider Scott and Julie a friend. They have that effect on people.

Another dual sport legend, and the creator of the Trans-America Trail Ride, Sam Correro, has also ridden a variety of dual sport motorcycles over the course of his long and amazing dual sport career. I'd bet, he enjoyed them all.

Me, I like simple. A Yamaha WR250R is simple enough that I can figure it out. A Suzuki DR650 I can also figure out. Likewise, a KLR 650, DRZ400, and others. Personally, I have no experience with KTM but after having ridden one, I can verify that the suspension was nothing short of supernatural and it sure was fun and likely easier to maintain than I expect.

Currently a trend is two-cylinder dual sport machines like the Yamaha Tenere 700, a fabulous motorcycle I'm sure, hard to come by and by the time it's outfitted and ready for that long ride, the price tag is simply more that I desire to periodically drop in the gravel of the roads upon which I ride. And, no way am I taking one over Black Bear Pass in Colorado. You might do so. I'm not. It's too pretty to scratch and it's too heavy. For me. Maybe not for you.

You will find one motorcycle too hot, another too cold, and one will be just right. Until time and boredom change your definitions of hot and cold.

There is another factor that drives my own personal dual sport decision. Resale value. A personal quirk of mine, some would say, personality flaw, is that I just can't bring myself to buy a new motorcycle, ride it, say three years and sell it at a price causes me to lose halve its purchase price.

I have purchased only one new motorcycle in my life and I'm still annoyed at myself about it.

The year was 1998.

A dealer in Atlanta, Georgia had a silver and red 1997 Moto Guzzi California 75th anniversary that had sat on his floor for over a year. He knew a drooling sucker when he saw one. He let me ride it, after which, the conversation went something like this.

Me. "I really like it, but there is a long ride I'm wanting to make that starts in Medford, Oregon and finishes in San Diego, California and I hate to ride all the way out to Medford on it.

Him. "I'll ship it to Medford. No cost. "

Me. "That might work, but I really should sell the 1994 BMW R100R that I bought from you last year before I buy this Guzzi."

Him. "I'll give you what you paid me for it on trade."

Me. "Does it come with those Hepco Becker hard bags sitting next to it?"

Him. "Today, it does, yes, it does."

The ride from Medford, on that Moto Guzzi, west to the Oregon Coast, south ward along the coastal highway, down to San Diego, to this day, is one of my best memories. I made the ride with a friend, he on his BMW cruiser, a capable, if contemporary styled motorcycle.

The Guzzi was a very unusual combination of style, power, handling, comfort (once the seat was changed) and character that I have not attained since. Although a Honda XR650R came danged close. I sold the Guzzi two years later. Then, under sad circumstances, it found its way back, not into my own life, but to the friend from the Oregon ride. He owns it still.

It was, and is, a fabulous motorcycle. All these years later, I don't regret the ride, but the money I lost on depreciation, still haunts me. I can't help it.

Maybe the best things in life, even memories, are meant to come at a cost.

Back to dual sport motorcycles.

Why did I choose an older Suzuki DR650 on the Conditional Divide? Because it's the bike I owned at the time. If I had spent time worrying and reasoning over another and maybe better motorcycle, I likely would not have made the trip. And, just like that long Guzzi ride down the coast, this ride has become one of my favorite memories.

What is that saying? Time waits for no man. A cliché but a cliché for a reason. Get out your own map. Go over your own motorcycle. Put on a new set of tires. Change all the fluids. Fuss over it. What then? Well, then, pick a date. Ship the bike if necessary. Either to the start of your ride or back home after the ride. Ride the darned thing if you have time, to the beginning of your ride, and back home. Take the back roads. Go slow. Go semi fast. Just go.

We now re-join our regularly scheduled program. The ride itself.

On the road to Canada, how did I arrive at World War II?

I leave the tie-dye blonde behind. Reluctantly. I hook up the camper to the truck and drive thirty-five miles north to Montrose.

The plan was to ride pavement from Ridgway to the Canadian border. Then to hop on the Continental Divide route and ride south.

I park my truck and the camper at a storage lot in Montrose, unload the DR650 from its ramp on the back and off I go.

I will return in about three weeks. In total, I will have ridden about sixteen hundred miles of pavement and two thousand miles of dirt.

Dirt is welcomed on this motorcycle. The pavement was not a fun thought. Compared to riding a horse or pedaling or walking, sure, it was a piece of cake, but after years of riding pavement on larger motorcycles designed for the task, one tends to get spoiled.

Then I realize.

I'm not on a time sensitive mission here. The weather won't be an issue.

An idea forms.

I decide to visit a place I've read about and wanted to see. Why not now? After checking that box, I can then ride to the Canadian Border.

So, off I go. To Creede, Colorado, an old mining town, now a tourist destination. Tucked back into a canyon, like Telluride only smaller, Creede is another must see for anyone riding Western Colorado. The town center is near the headwaters of the Rio Grande River, a blue-ribbon trout river.

The short cut to Creede from Ridgway is a 4x4 road over Uncompahgre Peak. This motorcycle can easily handle the route, but I decide to take pavement instead. My knowledge of the off-road route isn't sufficient to take the chance and I don't want to take the time to do the research. Pavement it shall be.

I leave the camper and truck to fend for themselves and hop on highway 50 riding East at fifty miles an hour. Soon I am in Cimarron, remaining on highway 50 through Sapinero at the Curecanti National Recreation Area, where I hang a right and take 149, a good motorcycle road, into Lake City, another old mining town, now an off-road enthusiast destination.

I pause for lunch, watching all types of 4x4, side by side, single seat ATV and dual sport motorcycles use the town as a fueling station to ride the high mountain trails, left behind from the mining days.

Marilyn is envious of the off road riding but agrees to my pavement plan. We take what has to be one of Colorado's most scenic roads, highway 149, gaining altitude then descending into Creede.

Creede did not disappoint. Quaint comes to mind. The three hundred people who reside year-round probably object to that word. I should ask a local for the word they would use. On the summer day I rode through, the temperature was seventy-five. Winters call for a hearty individual, the mercury dipping to twenty below.

When standing on main street and looking towards the canyon walls, one has the feeling the street is going to keep narrowing until it threads a needle into the canyon.

On the way into town from Lake City, about two miles outside of town center, there is a very long airstrip. It appears to be public. This has me scratching my head. A town this small with such a large air strip? Someone here really wanted that runway. Someone with the means and connections to make it happen.

Marilyn does not need a long runway, I've heard a DR650 can get airborne in a mere hundred feet. I'm not going to test it.

I'm feeling a tad too much grounded myself, so coffee is in order. I spot a restaurant with an outdoor seating area; Kip's is the name.

Kip's has fine coffee and finer tacos. Sitting here, in this historic town, on this sunny day, after riding highway 149 past alpine lakes, through high meadows, along the Rio Grande and into this place, I feel fortunate. A Thesaurus provides a few other words for this. They all apply. Blessed, lucky, destined.

Now, it's time for a "you have got to be kidding me" moment.

I didn't see it riding in, but on the way into Creede, just before reaching the air strip is an excellent lodge with riverside cabins and a restaurant. It's called "Antlers".

As mentioned, I now sit at a restaurant called "Kip's Bar and Grill."

In five years', time, from this moment, I am destined to return to Creede, spend the entire summer and play music at both Antlers and Kip's? If you had told me that then, sitting at Kip's before beginning the Continental Divide Ride, I wouldn't have believed you.

You can't make this stuff up.

One evening, during that summer, at Antlers, taking a break from singing, I say hello to a three people at a table.

A couple, named Robert and Krickett and a man named John.

Three things then happen.

First, Krickett is talked into singing a song she wrote about falling down in trout streams. It deserves an Emmy for funniest song about trout fishing and slippery river rocks. Every fisherman has at one time or another, busted his butt on slippery rocks.

Second, John is coerced into later bringing his beautiful Martin Guitar to play rhythm on a couple of tunes. He and his wife Ann have made Creede their summer home for twenty years. It's that kind of place. People tend to return.

Third.......

The year was 1954.

A painting is released. Immediately it's a huge hit. The artist is already well known. His works have captured the American experience for a decade now. The artist is Norman Rockwell, and this painting is his latest gem.

The painting is called "Breaking Home Ties"

It depicts a boy sitting next his father on a bench at a train station. The boy has a look of expectation. The father looks otherwise. A train ticket hangs from the boy's pocket. A suitcase with the emblem, "State U." is by his side. The man, cigarette hanging from the corner of his mouth, is dressed in blue labor clothes and he works the edges of a hat with his fingers. His leg touches his sons, but he is not looking at his son, knowing it's probably the right thing, this college thing, but also knowing he doesn't want him to go.

A dog sits with his head on the boy's knee, he too is sad, sensing the departure.

But none of it is true.

Yes, on that day, a painting was being contemplated. A boy was actually sitting next to a man. However, the man was not his father. There was no dog. The boy was not heading off to college. He had just happened to be at the right place when Mr. Rockwell was contemplating a new painting. The entire scene was set up.

Reality needs imagination. Imagination that resulted in a painting which appeared on the Cover of The Saturday Evening Post. The original painting would later sell for over a million dollars.

Why do I know all this?

Because on the deck of Antlers, with his wife, sits Robert, the boy in the painting. Sixty-six years have passed since the painting was released. Robert laughs at the craziness of how things turn out. We both laugh at reality and imagination.

I ask him if he would mind sitting still tomorrow for about thirty minutes while I hire a local artist to sketch his image. I'll add luggage and a dog later. Maybe we can sell it.

Robert. "What should we write on the luggage instead of State U; maybe a decal for the AARP?"

Do yourself a favor, book a stay with Antlers, owned by Chuck and Patti Powers. While in Creede, enjoy both their restaurant and also take the time to dine at Kip's, owned by, yes, Kip. He and Kerry will treat you well. I hope to see you at both places.

Bring your original Norman Rockwell painting. Trade it for a log home in Creede with acreage and an airplane. Live in the cabin. Land the plane on that a nice long runway just down the road.

Back to our story. The Continental Divide awaits.

I spend the night in Creede, unaware of my future, and hit the road early. Well, early for me, ten AM. Two hundred ninety miles later I reach Meeker, Colorado.

Small dual sport motorcycles can offer a comfort of sorts. Compared to a pogo stick, they are quite luxurious. The map towards the Canadian border, hoping to avoid most expressway travel, took me from Creede, northward through a small town in Colorado named Meeker. Meeker isn't exactly on the way to the border, but I wanted to see the town. The map made it look like a piece of cake. And compared to walking, it was.

I take a moment to walk around the lovely courthouse square, where I meet a retired Marine.

He prefers to remain nameless. As we chatted, he pointed with obvious pride towards a statue on square. A statue he had been instrumental in having placed there. It is one of the earliest memorials in the United States to soldiers who served in WWII.

Riding through small towns one can easily miss these sorts of encounters. Like often happens, when traveling on a motorcycle he notices the Suzuki, giving common ground among two strangers.

"What type of bike is that?" he asks

"It's a street legal dirt bike, made by Suzuki, a single cylinder, electric start bike that prefers dirt. It's just punished me for riding pavement from Ridgway to here. " Says me.

"You don't say." He says, looking it over.

"It ain't for everybody." I toss that out.

"Maybe when I was younger." He offers.

"There are a lot of maybes when we were younger." I say.

We laugh. Each content in our own grey hair.

"See that statue over there?" he asks.

"I saw it riding in, it's why I stopped. "

"Me and some friends, saw to putting it there."

And he tells the story of honor. A desire to honor those who fought. Those who came home. And those who did not. He is rightly proud.

We sit for a moment, talking of nothing at all, and of everything there is to share. He too fought. His time, his moment in history, different than my own. Purely due to birth date. Nothing more. He and his generation did not have a choice in history. The sheer numbers and economic power of this country, thankfully, ensured freedom from truly terrible tyranny. His generation rose to the challenge.

"That statue will be that last of us standing," he says.

I didn't know what to say. So, I looked over at him, held out my hand, shook his and said, "Thank you."

Semper Fi, sir. Semper Fi, indeed.

After a pause in Meeker, I press on to the Canadian border, riding like a man possessed. Interstate miles pile up. Knobby tires wear down. Mental state mostly survives.

There is very little reward in riding small motorcycles on interstate highways. It's mostly an endurance contest. The single cylinder motor drones on and on. And on. And on. It drones until one's mind and throttle hand scream like a child whose mother won't let it touch every single thing in the grocery store.

Highway miles suck. Screaming kids suck. There is a correlation there somewhere, but it eludes me. I'd consider it more carefully, but my mind and my ass are numb.

Shut up and ride.

Drone. Drone. Drone.

A tiny but highly annoying muscle spasm has worked its way up my right arm, into my right shoulder. Old dual sport motorcycles do not have cruise control. The tiny effort necessary to hold the throttle open has a large effect on small muscles.

I shake my arm. This does no good. I roll my shoulder. This also does no good. I slow down and stand on the pegs. This does no good either but does receive a stare from the man in a car next to me.

I wonder if Rooster Cogburn bitched about holding his reins all day.

Since leaving Ridgway, I have filled my hand not with bad-guy-terminating 2nd amendment issue, but rather with throttle, clutch and brake. Rooster Cogburn would likely laugh if he were to saddle up from the grave, but surely even old Rooster took leave at times to ride for the sake of the ride. Even his chestnut quarter horse, once in a while, carried him into the clarity of wild lands for no purpose at all, which is one of the greatest purposes of all.

I'm completely and totally burnt out. Self-induced monotony. Towns came and towns went. Montrose, Grand Junction, Meeker, Green River, Provo, Salt Lake City. Northward still to Cherry Creek, Pocatello, Idaho Falls, Red Rock, Butte, Clearwater, past Salmon Lake State Park, and Swan Lake, at last through Kalispell and Eureka.

The journey so far has been mostly four lane divided interstate, something this motorcycle will tolerate, but does not enjoy. Something this rider will tolerate but also does not enjoy.

My demeanor slowly deteriorating. Plodding. Enduring. One large cylinder thumping in a rhythm more in semblance to the vibration of a snare drum than the soothing beat of a Harley Davidson. Ain't no perfect motorcycle. Ain't no perfect road. Ain't no perfect route and there ain't no sunshine when she's gone.

Pavement Day Idaho Hwy 26

Too much of a good thing? When, exactly does that moment occur?

Maybe it's just a natural extension of any endeavor. I recall last October, riding the 5200-mile Trans-America Trail, I was approximately halfway between Tennessee and Oregon when I hit a wall. Figuratively.

Today. Same feeling. Enough. So, with the Snake River as my guide, Marilyn and I take it easy along one hundred fifty miles of mostly aimless wandering along its banks, on highway 26, Idaho.

We take a long lunch then a longer coffee break. We sat for a spell and watched the river run its course. I never tire of water. Western rivers. Coastal marsh. Bahama blue. It doesn't matter. Norman McLean, describing his life, hit a nail squarely with his famous phrase, "and a river runs through it".

Tomorrow is another day to make trail miles. Today, the Snake River surges it's meandering blue green current like voltage through an extension cord to recharge the inner batteries.

Along the way, I spot a trike pulling a trailer, and am reminded of the expression, "you can't take everything you need."

Well, maybe you can.

As I write these paragraphs, I wonder why. Why did I take to the wide highways and rush to the Canadian border? What was to be gained? I recall some misplaced worry about weather. I recall wanting to gain the beginning of the ride. When, in fact, there is no real beginning as surely as there is no real ending.

I realize that a label had moved me to make such a rushed decision to ride from Colorado to the Canadian border, to ride fast and blind instead of slowly and seeing.

A label called "The Great Continental Divide Ride."

Imagine if a previous rider had mapped a gravel road route from Ridgway, Colorado to Roosville, British Columbia, started a website and sold copies of the route and named it "The Great Route to Roosville."

Hundreds of lemmings, like myself would have likely risen to the challenge. The beginning of my ride would have been within single digit miles of that Ridgway coffee shop. In fact, two rides would have been possible. Two goals with one stone. Ridgway to Canada. Then, Canada to Mexico.

With a few hours of free wi-fi, I could have created just such a ride from Ridgway. I'm retired. There was no rush. Except the self-inflicted sort.

Still, the goal of reaching the Canadian border has been accomplished.

The temperature at the Canadian border is slightly colder than those I've experienced for the past three days, colder than was Ridgway, even though the altitude here at the border is six thousand feet lower.

Coordinates of longitude and latitude aren't something to which a motorcycle rider usually pays much attention. An onboard GPS takes care of such navigation, rendering the need for charts, sextants, plotting and pencil unnecessary. Early navigators like Captain Cook would have given their scurvy laden best crew for such a marvel.

Marilyn is running smoothly. Of this fact, I am somewhat amazed. She has carried myself and luggage from that coffee shop, northward, through a multiple of altitudes. It's the changing of altitude which I had expected to be an issue. Marilyn is not fuel injected. She has a far older fuel system, namely a carburetor. Carburetors are notoriously finicky about altitude changes.

Gore-Tex outerwear layered over fleece or wool keeps the comfort in check, but the altitude wreaks havoc on carburetors. The science behind Gore-Tex and carburetors may not be as exciting as say a perfectly executed electric guitar version of Eric Clapton's Layla; but, six string wizardry aside, those who invented waterproof outerwear and carburetors are every bit as talented as Slowhand himself.

Gore-Tex and carbs share one thing in common. Atmosphere. Moisture, air molecules, pressure and the tiny changes of each one become important as one wanders among different elevations.

The higher the elevation, the less column of air there is above us, and therefore less pressure and therefore less oxygen. Because Oxygen can be compressed. Like in a scuba tank. A lot of oxygen in a little space. Resembling an understated guitar solo, it's all about the mix.

Describing the inner workings of a motorcycle and its fuel system is nowhere near as interesting as speaking of the curvature of well-fitting cut off blue jean shorts, but here it goes...

A carburetor is designed to mix just the right amount of oxygen with just the right amount of fuel. This is done with small openings called jets. The larger the opening in the jet, the more fuel it allows to flow. However, since there is less oxygen at high altitudes, that same amount of fuel is now mixed with less oxygen, thus messing up the ratio of fuel to oxygen.

Long story short, the motorcycle runs poorly, has less power, as if the sound stage manager pulled the plug halfway into the song just as the backup singer hit the high note.

Luckily smart people have figured out a solution to keep the carb concert flowing. Change the jet opening to one that is smaller, thus restoring the correct ratio of fuel to air. A smaller opening allows less fuel which is then mixed with the high altitude less air. The theoretical guitar player is once again happy. He and the backup singer are now both on key.

To avoid the perils of carbs, smart people invented electronic fuel monitors, and a fuel injection system. This system, in modern automobiles and in modern motorcycles make tiny adjustments to fuel air mixture ratios. New motorcycles are mostly fuel injected.

Today's fuel injection is highly reliable. At most, the fuel pump may fail. Fuel pumps are easily replaced and readily available.

When was the last time you were on a ride with friends and someone's fuel injection failed? Yea, me neither. Just like it is prudent to take tools on a long ride, it may also be prudent to pack a spare fuel pump, if your ride takes you into places where one is not likely to be found. Say, like the Sahara Desert. In the States, the worst-case scenario is sitting at a camp site for a couple of days waiting on Amazon.

Note to self, next time, buy a fuel injected motorcycle. Oh, yea, and a 1960's Stratocaster. But I already own this sterling example of a DR650.

To further prove that I'm a slow learner, today, several years after attempting the Continental Divide ride, what do I own? A 1995 Harley Davidson Heritage Softail. With a carburetor. And yes, the carburetor has been wrestled off the bike, cleaned, re-jetted and wrestled back on.

In another example of wrestling, the farm lobby succeeded in pinning a few politicians to the mat. The result of which was that farmers now supply 10 percent of our fuel with corn-based ethanol.

Ethanol added to gasoline may keep farmers happy, but it wreaks havoc on the tiny jets in motorcycle carburetors. Studies have shown that ethanol attracts water. Studies have also shown that the ethanol and gasoline begin to separate in as little as three weeks. Combine water attraction with separation and the ethanol gas mix inside your tank turns to a mess. Mess is a technical term for all of us who flunked college chemistry.

Whatever we call it, the resulting brew clogs those tiny carb jets. Like most things, I learned this the hard way, leaving ethanol gas inside the gas tank for several months at a time, and then wondered why the motorcycle wouldn't start.

Riding the motorcycle every day, on rides like this one, keep the moisture and separation at bay. Other problems arise, as we will see later, but ethanol sludge isn't one of them.

I wonder what unforeseen issues will arrive with lithium? Maybe the rechargeable batteries will cost more to recycle than to produce. I read that Princeton is working on a way to remove the copper, cobalt, nickel and manganese in a cost-effective manner. There are very smart people in this world.

Two days of wondering about my own smarts and two days of whining later. I arrive at the Canadian border. The tiny muscle atop my right shoulder still suffers, but now it speaks to me with a different accent. Eh?

The ride begins..........

Day 1

Canadian Border (Roosville) to Eureka, MT...

Today I discover that leaves enjoy cleavage.

But first, I made it. Finally. To the official start of this ride.

Ridgway is long gone. Left in the rear-view mirror three days ago. Three long days of pavement pounding. Thankfully behind me.

While I fret over carb jets, Marilyn is parked in the grass, ten feet to the side of route 93 in northern Montana. I stand alongside, taking in the scene. Her frame is dusty and unkept. Her tires show the flat wear of long miles on pavement. The red piping along the edges of the navy-blue seat more resembles rustic brown spray paint than the purity of crimson that once was. My own grimy blue riding suit blends well with the bike. We are both a sore sight. Attire and attitude alike have suffered the penalty of road miles on a small motorcycle.

Pointing the cell phone camera at the motorcycle, I notice its difficulty in adopting to the low light of late afternoon. The photo will likely be underexposed. The flash will never reach far enough to take in the scene. I allow this little annoyance to play a larger role in my state of mind than it should, cussing technology, cussing carb jets and flogging myself at being such a cell phone cheap skate.

While looking at the photo, I notice the swath of grey duct tape along the upper section of the plastic visor. It's a life saver while riding towards the setting sun. Just lower my head slightly and it becomes a sun visor.

I need a coffee. I need a better cell phone camera. I need a tied-dyed lass with whom to laugh. I need a bath.

The photo burns into the cell phone memory and into my own, an image. Framing the U.S.; Canadian border in the background. The scene is commiserating and commemorating the blessed end of pavement. It may be almost dark, but it's time to begin the Great Continental Divide Ride. Or at least the first twenty miles.

I have arrived, tired as I may be. The beginning has begun.

Gathering mobile phone and mental momentum, I saddle up and ride south, the GPS piloting me towards an easy twenty-mile gravel section that runs west of route 93.

Suddenly there are no more cars, no more worry about one of them turning left in front of me, to later say "I didn't see you." One of the fears of all motorcycle riders. Many of us make a slight weave, a slight movement designed to catch the eye of the driver of the car, to avoid just such "I didn't see you", tragedy. Many times, the motorcyclist is no longer around to hear the "I didn't see you."

The pace slows. The mind focuses. The air becomes somehow more crisp. As I write this sentence, the word processor does not like "more crisp". It's determined to alter my word to "crispier." I'll stick with more crisp. So, the air, being more crisp, is also more nicer, much more nicer. In the span of five minutes, nothing has changed and everything has changed. Word processors don't know shite.

Like a marathon runner busting through "the wall", I am regenerated into a world of slower moving scenery. Scenery I notice instead of scenery passing by peripheral vision where it is neither recognized nor embraced. Shrubs and trees and the shape of bark come into clarity.

The scent of a forest draughts through my helmet. Rocky Mountain Juniper. Ponderosa Pine. Lodgepole pine. The forest is alive. The motorcycle is alive. *I* am alive.

Gone are the fast-moving cars, intent projectiles embracing equally intent occupants. Replaced by the sound of this small motorcycle, its tires rolling over gravel and welcome slow speed induced air passing into the raised visor of my helmet, along sunglasses, careening as gentle wind will do into and onto, until who knows where it goes.

Behind those sunglasses, for the first time in three days, I smile and laugh out loud. Everything has changed. More nicer.

Too soon, the gravel road lands me back onto Route 93 and into downtown Eureka where I will seek a simple meal and a simple hotel.

Later I learn that Eureka, originally known as Deweyville, has a history as a logging town and a provider of Spruce Christmas Trees and before that, the early inhabitants grew a strain of tobacco giving it the nick name of Tobacco Valley.

Today, there are less than fifteen hundred full time inhabitants, owed likely to its remoteness, the end of logging and a rather chilly seventeen-degree January average low.

Tourist, like myself find it quaint and charming and chilly.

I pull into a small café, park the bike, remove gloves, remove helmet, place helmet over mirror, think twice, remove helmet from mirror, take it in hand and walk inside. I've watched helplessly as more than one helmet fell from the mirror perch.

A menu on the wall, again in white chalk on a black chalk board, touts freshly made sandwiches and baked goods.

The brunette behind the counter looks up as I approach. She is about five-nine, one twenty, easily New York runway model material.

She wears black knee length tapered shorts and a black tee shirt, cut low. The shirt fell only to her navel, revealing just enough to pose a question about the rest.

A hint of grey shows along one temple. She wears a tightly woven cotton apron proudly displaying the name of the establishment. She carries herself well, slender with impressive posture.

A sterling bangle in the shape of a silver leaf hangs from each ear, pulled together nicely with a short silver chain around her neck to which is suspended a silver pendant, also in the shape of a leaf. Her left wrist is surrounded by another silver chain, with a solitary charm. Yep, it too was a leaf.

My highly trained skills of deduction tell me she liked trees.

"What can I get started for you?" she asks.

"Has the whole world adopted the Starbucks mantra?" I say. I didn't mention the leaves but wanted to.

"I worked at one for a year. It's a habit. I must have said it a million times during that year."

Her expression was one of raised eyebrows, rolled eyes and slightly shaking head, poking fun at herself with no sign of embarrassment. I liked that. Then she flashed an impressive smile. I guessed that smile could achieve whatever ends it desired. She could single handedly save every leaf on every tree in the world with that smile. Or lobby for the timber industry.

"I bet you did." I still didn't mention the leaves. But, still wanted to.

I see her gaze at my blue jacket. Her head rose slightly and words almost formed, but her mind changed.

I beat her to the punch.

I pointed to my jacket and pants. "Bought all of this at a yard sale last year. I think the guy selling it worked for a blueberry factory."

"Hope you got a good deal." She was quick.

"He almost gave it to me."

"He was a smart man." She was very quick.

Oh, how I wanted to mention the leaves.

I settled on a laugh, and silently wondered if she knew of Shrek.

She handed me a square flat thin object which resembled a drink coaster except it has a row of blinking red lights, flashing in a formation that I once saw on an airport runway, at night.

I took it.

"It will buzz when your sandwich is ready." She says.

"Will it fly off on its own or should I bring it back to you?"

"No, silly, bring it up here and pick your food up at the counter." She pointed to her left.

"Ah, OK, will do."

Finding a quiet table in a corner, I find myself once again thankful. For this ride. For simple and good food. For women with humor. She had been willing to laugh at herself and at the world. We need more of that. Life is short. It shouldn't all be thousand-mile torture rides. Unexpectedly I didn't even mind the over used Starbucks slang. Instead, I found myself contemplating more interesting uses.

I imagine God, at the very moment one is born, looking down from divinity and asking.

"What can I get started for you?"

After guessing at God's good humor, I locate a small hotel, plop on the bed and with Wi-Fi that is slower than a near-sighted IRS agent auditing a

billionaire's tax return, I read of one of the first
Europeans to set foot along the Continental Divide.

The year was 1514.

A boy was born in Basque County, Spain. His
uncle was a politician. Of his early life, not much is
written. He learned well from his social climbing uncle
and the boy, when reaching the years of a young man,
married the daughter of a rich conquistador, and over
the course of his life would father eight children.

In 1533, before all the children, at the age of
nineteen, he made the long ocean passage to what is
today southern Mexico, at the time, due to Spanish
control, was called New Spain. Another Spanish
gentleman who also was wedded to a rich wife,
Coronado, was also in New Spain.

Coronado sought gold. He recruited the boy into
the cause. The boy was Juan de Zaldivar.

Juan and Coronado were not the first Spaniards
to enter New Spain, but they were likely the first to
travel so far north into today's Colorado.

Juan had a fever. Gold Fever. Juan was also
driven like young men everywhere to make a reputation
for himself. At the behest of Coronado, he and a team
suffered mightily as they rode horseback near the
Continental Divide, as far north as the San Luis Valley,
Colorado. The men traversed game trails, and Indian
trails.

Their mission was to locate what would turn out
to be only a myth, the City of Cibola, supposedly full of
gold. Financing the exploits of Spain was costing the

rulers massive amounts of coin and they desperately needed more.

The San Luis Valley rests on the eastern decent of the Continental Divide, covering both eight-thousand square miles and the broken dreams of Juan de Zaldivar.

No pity should be extended his way. By 1566, historians believe he owned mines and farms and was one of the wealthiest men in New Spain.

He died in 1670, at the age of fifty-six, having nary a clue that people like me would ride motorcycles on the same Continental Divide.

We do so on paths he once rode on horseback.

We would do so in leisure, no kingdom demanding we find gold, no higher-ranking officer pushing us into the unknown.

Day 2

Today, my good nature is tested, and I see the world through a young boy's eyes.

Breakfast in Eureka is a Cliff bar and hotel coffee. I am in no hurry. Checkout time is 11am. It's only 8:30. My travel style can best be called slow and slower.

Sipping coffee laced with hard caked packets of fake creamer isn't nearly as rewarding as tall witty Bob

Seger brunettes. At least the room came equipped with a miniscule coffee maker and three slim sachets of coffee, likely older than the bedspread and maybe not as stale. One was decaf. I tossed it in the trash.

For a moment, I consider suiting up and riding the bike to a restaurant. Anyone who has traveled by motorcycle will understand the hesitance. Going to breakfast on a motorcycle takes effort. Effort with far more steps than getting dressed and strolling to the car. It's a motorcycle thing.

First, pack the street clothes into your luggage. Second, don the motorcycle attire. Third, walk to the motorcycle while balancing the helmet, the luggage and an armored jacket. Fourth, hoist said luggage and pack it on the bike, while either wearing the helmet or hanging it on the mirror, where it will do its best to lose its balance and hit the ground, whereupon, fifth, you remember this quaint fact and place it on the ground, because if you don't, you are highly likely to utter your first cuss word of the day, because you know better, but hung it there anyway.

Finally, sixth, you put on gloves and then put on the helmet, whereupon you notice that you can't buckle the helmet with gloves on, so you do, now, utter your first foul word of the day because, yes, you know better, so you take off the gloves, buckle the helmet, and once again, put on the gloves.

Car travelers, you don't know what you're missing.

I can't bring myself to make steps one through six, so crummy creamer it is.

Yesterday was a long day, full of blueberry jokes, blackish blue pavement and the sounds of blue clear air through my helmet.

I am almost ready to ride. The bike is parked outside and eager. No DR650 needs caffeine. It needs spark, fuel, compression and oxygen, but no caffeine. It's mechanical. I am not. I do need fuel and oxygen, but my spark and compression are provided by outside sources, one of which is food.

A Cliff bar comes to the rescue.

This morning, resting on a modern mattress I use a sketchy internet to travel backwards and to read of people who slept on mats. I also read of wind. One that blew a slow but steady change from East to West, much of that change occurring within miles of where the motorcycle is parked.

The year was 10,000 B.C.

Three hundred and fifty miles south east of this hotel, a male infant is buried by his Anzick family.

His name will never be known. He did not reach man hood. Instead, he made history.

His grave was discovered in 1968 near Willsall, Montana at what is known as the Anzick 1 site.

Genome studies, completed in 2014, show him to be a descendant of Asians. Carbon dating reveals he is likely to have died twelve thousand years ago. At that moment, he becomes one of the oldest known inhabitants of North America.

Later discoveries in South America reveal another theory of the first to arrive, perhaps as long as fifteen thousand years ago.

No matter the scientific truth, one human truth permeates all time. His family, like families everywhere who have suffered such tragic loss, has to go on without him.

Centuries later, family and tribal perseverance blend to become the Crow tribe.

Nine thousand years after the death of that boy, another boy, a descendent of the Anzick, now in his early teens, crouches behind a rocky outcropping near the lower Yellowstone River.

It is summer. His last meal was yesterday midday, consisting of berries and bitterroot. He knows which berries are safe and which will make him sick, which may kill him. His people, over centuries learned these facts the same way humans throughout the ages learn most lessons, the hard way.

The days are long at this time of year.

He has waited for this moment, late in the long day. He knows this is the best time. He knows this because his elders taught him. They did so by taking him with them on their own outings, using whatever cover the land provided, sometimes lying flat on the ground. They lay there for as long as it took.

The young man does not want to disappoint those back at the encampment. He does not want to disappoint the growing image he has of himself. His place within the Crow people.

He had practiced. He knew much could go wrong. A loud misstep. A small branch could, and has in his past, ricochet his projectile astray. His stomach knots, both from an inadequate diet and from nerves. Killing is necessary. Killing is also brutal. The food nourishes. The killing does not.

Perhaps this is why his tribe and future generations have almost a reverence for and give thanks for the food.

His prey is motionless, its eyes turn away from the young man. It is time. He rises slightly, draws the bow and the arrow flies. No branch interferes. He will eat well tonight.

He takes the game back to the encampment. His tribe is part of a community, of approximately six thousand souls spread out over large portions of land.

I traveled to this area on two wheels. Their transport at the time would have been limited to two feet. Spanish explores had just begun to bring horses to North America. Walking limited the range of nomadic movement, but still they remarkably covered almost three million acres, moving as seasons changed. Today's tourist, like myself, easily cover a distance in two days that would have taken the Crow two months.

Daily life was hard. Life spans were short.

Like the other western tribes, they used seasonal homes to take advantage of the resources available during each season, almost always returning to the same location each year.

In the late 1700's French trappers traded with native Americans but were few numbers having no displacing influence on the tribe

The continent was scattered with tribe after tribe, each carving out their own territory through war and the relative openness of space. Even with such a low population there were clashes among the tribes, many routinely engaging in brutal acts of kidnapping, slavery and torture.

Mainly, though, the simple demands of daily life ruled. Unless threatened with attack, humans everywhere must find food, water and shelter. The Crow was primarily dependent upon hunting, fishing and foraging for wild plants and roots. Women were predominantly responsible for the gathering of plants and roots.

Men hunted, fished and defended the tribe from its tribal enemies when necessary.

I close the computer and ready for the day.

I've rested, showered and even shaved. My motorcycle is still a dusty mess. For a very brief second, I consider finding a self-serve car wash, then decide against it. Eureka may not have such a place and it's almost 10:30 am. There are miles to ride. I can put up with a dirty dual sport.

Sorry Marilyn, I'll try not to let anyone you know see you.

I check the tires, the chain, the brake and turn signal lights and the headlight. All is well. Then I check the weather. All is well there also. No rain in the forecast. There has been no rain in a week, so the gravel roads, over which I will pass today will be like riding on easy street. The temperature is moderate.

I saddle up, turn the key, press the start button, sending voltage to the starter and Marilyn comes to life. She breaths a kind and quiet cadence. Today will be like that, nothing harsh. No hard charging. No excess throttle. I promise myself to ride like a canoe down a slow and winding river, eyeing the foreground and the forest for whatever may come.

The route presses southward, once again on a smooth gravel lane and like yesterday parallel and east of Highway 93. Soon, however the route alters course, heading almost due east, where it intersects with Highway 93 where the route turns right to cruise along 93 southwards on pavement for a few miles before turning left onto Grave Creek Road, and riding northeast, again on pavement through rural, low populated northern Montana.

The road turns to dirt and meanders through forest and alongside the creek from which it takes its name. At some point, the road changes name to national forest 114 bearing almost due north, then north west, and finally curving southward.

If a rider were to pay attention to compass direction during this section, he would swear that a mistake had been made. Why would such a route take a line that runs almost directly to the north, when the Continental Divide runs north to south? The answer lies in the land itself, and the task of road construction following contour lines of topography. A path directly north to south is impossible in places, this being one of them. Following creeks requires less dynamite, tunnels and bulldozers. So north we go, then east, then finally, the land allows for a southerly direction.

Bald Mountain will appear to the north, then fade from sight, the route following this creek, then that creek, each with names given from the history of the area. Yakinikak, Lewis, Ketchikan and others. The riding is easy. The roads smooth.

This Suzuki DR650, with so few miles under its wheels and such outstanding maintenance by its previous owner, is flawless. Even with a stock suspension, I'm comfortable and in control. Granted at my slow speeds, I'm not exactly taxing the limits of its far east designers.

The route turns south and Nasukoin mountain can be seen to the west, the tallest peak in the Whitefish range, at just over eight thousand feet.

Early in the day as the miles pile on, the land changes, remodeling itself every twenty miles or so.

Personally, a slow inner remodeling begins to take shape. Without plans or drawings, without a hammer or a nail or a carpenter's level, the long days of panoramic riding build their own inner structure which says "slow down, take a moment here, a moment there, ease up on the throttle as this scene becomes another and another.

Listen to streams and rivers that flow now and flowed then, as those carrying bow and arrow camped along this river or in that meadow, unsure of making their own destination, unsure of tomorrow, listening to movement of water and what their currents may bring.

Remembering my own reasons, I put aside historical context, and ride as smoothly as I am able.

By two in the afternoon, the route reaches scenic Whitefish Lake, and soon thereafter the town of Whitefish where I pause for a diet coke and find a bench in the shade.

Resting, content in the knowledge that I've ridden an utterly unimpressive seventy-five or so miles since leaving the hotel just before eleven a.m., I realize why I'm never invited along for a group ride. Most dual sport guys would have been far down the road by now, fingers twitching for more. My own fingers barely contain their joy at holding a diet coke over crushed ice, content to hold it for another twenty or thirty minutes. Maybe I'll have another.

Just before entering the town of Whitefish, I had noticed a sign that said "Happy Haven".

That about sums it up.

My goal for the day, if I ever got up from this bench, and it's a very loosely held goal, is the village of Seeley Lake, which would produce about two hundred miles total riding. More than I usually ride in a day, but today, the miles are easy, many of them on pavement so average speed is high.

As I think of moving on from my seat in the shade, a mother and young boy walk by.

The boy sees a large bug splat on my jacket, which I hadn't noticed. He points at it.

"Wow!" he says.

I look down to view the splat, which is indeed massive. "It's ok, he didn't feel a thing." I say.

The boy grimaces and the Mom takes over. "But did you?" She asks.

I'm beginning to think all Montana women are quick witted.

"Nearly knocked me off the motorcycle, but my bullet proof vest saved me."

The boys jaw dropped. "Really, really, you have a bullet proof vest? Can I see it? Can I? "

The mother interjected. "You sound like you are from Texas."

"No ma'am, Georgia."

The boy again, "Can I see it?"

Mom, "He doesn't have a bullet proof vest, son, it's just silly and uneducated southern humor."

I almost said, "You cut me deep Shrek."

Unsure of what constituted silly uneducated southern humor, and not wanting to tell her what I really thought of the comment in front of her son, I took the easy way out. For a moment, I wished I carried a small laminated copy of my law degree. I'd show her, by God, uneducated, my ass!

A sip of diet coke and watching the boy, pure in his joy and exploration brought a dose of patience to my manner, suddenly realizing that prejudice comes in many forms, North and South, West and East, Black and White, Old and Young, Cars and Motorcycles.

I settled on "Well Ma'am, a professor of mine, long ago, who taught the finer points of Tort, told his class the story of a fly on a windshield of a car. The car might well be the aggressor and the fly has been duly and terminally wronged, yet what duty does the windshield owe to the fly and surely there was no intent to harm. But the relatives of the fly demand justice. Damages would be easily proven but difficult to define, and lessons for law students and children should probably be held to a higher standard than that of the windshield and the fly."

I looked the boy in the eye and gave him what his mother would not.

"Don't worry, Montana kids are tough. You don't need a vest to conquer bugs." I raised my diet coke in her son's direction, ignoring the mom, who needed ignoring.

He beamed. He seemed satisfied. Mom, for likely the first time in her mostly adult life was speechless, so she resumed walking, boy in tow, who was still looking back at the giant yellow and green splat, wondering, no doubt about bullet proof vests and Montana toughness.

Finding my own toughness, I eased the Styrofoam diet coke cup into the trash and make my way, hoping for wide roads and narrow bugs and women with uneducated southern humor.

Soon enough after a route that jigged left and jagged right, and somewhat to the south, Flathead Lake, all twenty-seven miles of it appears to my right. The lake is fifteen miles wide and three hundred seventy feet deep. In winter it must be a figurative three hundred seventy degrees below zero at its darkest reaches. I shiver at the thought of spending a winter here. Montana tough I am not.

Tough or not, there is a certain pace and cadence to riding a motorcycle over long distances. The first day, one is becoming accustomed to the seat, the reach of the handlebars, the cadence of the engine and a unique mindset which takes over.

A day-ride near one's home is a different thing entirely. Begin at home. End at home. For the most part, you know where you are going. You know where you have been. You know where you will end. This all sounds trivial. It is not.

During a long ride, you know where you have been, but you are not aware of it the same as you are aware of your home. Sure, you passed through, but it's still a bit of a mystery. And you ride through and towards another mystery, each mile encouraging another. And another. Until they add up in a series of snap shots playing slowing in your head. This creek. That slope of mountain. That confident sunlight opening the camera that is your eye to a visual interpretation to be witnessed at only the certain time of day during which you passed. Ride early or mid-day or late. The scene is different each time.

All of these influences make up a series of snap shots that you carry with you until the end of the day. In an attempt to remember the best of those scenes, you pull over and take a real photo with a real camera. The photo that will change the perspective due to the limitations of lens and light, creating another view entirely.

The mental snapshots become a movie. The road becomes a rhythm. The rhythm becomes the soundtrack to the film through which you ride. Curling one's right hand slightly speeds up the scene. Easing off has the effect of sharpening the focus.

Through it all, time alters, your eyes are fixated mostly ahead entering new world after new world, deciding which world to sharpen the focus and slow down. You are your own director, producer, cinematographer and actor. You decide when to say "action" and when to say "cut." Maybe there is an even more scenic river just around the next bend, so "action" it is. Maybe there is a small cafe with a cold diet coke and a curious boy simultaneously enamored and grossed out about giant bug guts, where the star will have the perfect line, well thought and well written by your own team of writers. Tough enough to withstand colossal bug spalts and to jump small creeks in a single bound.

I wonder if my own Continental Divide Ride mental movie will end with a sunset scene and a subdued sound track or parked alongside the road of those movies never to be released, never to find an audience and never to be heard from again. Something about this train of thought causes my mind to wander backwards, towards unobtainable ladies.

A few months ago, before traveling with my camper to Colorado, I had entered a black powder, round ball, target shooting contest. The contest was being held in northern Phoenix at one of the largest outdoor shooting facilities in the United States, Ben Avery Park.

The competition was divided into several categories. I had entered the one which makes use of smooth bore guns, ignited by a flintlock. My historical long gun was built using beautiful maple grain, presented with brass "furniture" and a single trigger, being of sixty caliber and a thirty-nine-inch smooth barrel with a single front sight. I was well equipped and fairly well practiced. Little did I know that the shooting competition was not the most interesting, nor the most appealing thing I was to witness. More on this later.

But interesting past events can wait. At the moment, I just want collect my thoughts and ride on. The route passes to the west of what is today the Lewis and Clark National Forest. The gravel turns east, then south, then east once more. Scenery is limited due to the height of the trees along the trail.

It's like that sometimes, riding through a forest provides no sense of scale to the natural features. One is unaware of altitude and vista. Attention is required. The condition of the gravel and dirt demand a certain respect, drawing one's eye away from what may be significant geography. There is time which can be taken to stop and look. But time is not unlimited. Miles, no matter how few, must be made.

With almost three million acres, the National Forest to my East is home to both black and brown bear. I have read that the paw print of a medium brown bear is larger than the footprint of a size 15 shoe. With claws. This is no place I wish to suffer a break down and subsequent overnight camp. Sure, the odds of a bear encounter are small, but I am even more sure the odds are smaller still in a Motel 6.

History has made its way into one of the flowers growing alongside this path as it exits the forest and emerges onto wider spaces. A light purple low-lying flower catches my eye. I didn't know at the time, but I was looking at the State flower of Montana, the bitterroot, also known as Lewisia rediviva. And, you guessed right, it's named after Merriweather Lewis.

I've ridden a hundred and fifty miles, with forty yet to ride. I locate a flat wide area and pull over to stretch. The range on this motorcycle with its large plastic tank, if ridden at an easy pace, is close to two hundred twenty miles. I check the fuel level. All is well. My own fuel level could use some topping off. The left front pocket of my jacket holds several Cliff bars. My right saddle bag holds a large bottle, filled with tea. Until this ride, I didn't realize that blueberry Cliff bars go rather well with tea. Then again, anything would go well with tea after a hundred and fifty miles of dirt.

Mount up. Hit the start button. Feel that relief when the bike fires to life. Attached to the cockpit area is a voltmeter. When riding, it reads between 13 and 14 volts. That is the happy section. If it should ever read less than 13 volts, that would be the sad section, meaning the battery wasn't charging properly and something must be done. All of you engineers out there would explain this in an entirely different manner, maybe speaking of absorption and sulphates and float. All I know is the happy section and the sad section.

The bike started. I'm happy.

I ride past huge Larch trees, which need the wet soil to thrive. Some, according to a Montana website, are over 600 years old.

The lake holds Rainbow Trout, Northern Pike, Walleye, Perch and more. I didn't test this knowledge. A DR650 is a poor choice to haul fishing rods.

Into the passage, I ride once more. I'm ready to be there. Seeley Lake, Montana. I'm ready to check in to a hotel and to find a quaint place for a quaint meal.

An hour later, I get my wish. I find both the room and the meal.

Day 3

Today, I will stumble across lingerie and romance. But first a man needs a good breakfast and coffee.

I awake finding myself in unsure surroundings. This happens sometimes on a long ride. I check the advertisements on the small desk in the room, and read Seeley Lake, Montana. Now I remember. There is a printed page letting its readers know that Seeley Lake is named for the first hearty settlers to build a cabin in the area, Jasper Seeley. And that Seeley Lake's first settlers were the Salish Indians.

Half asleep, I stroll down to the hotel breakfast area where coffee is served.

I grab two flyers from the rack next to the front desk. The first one assures me that in the Seeley Lake area the wildlife are still wild.

I'm not sure what to make of this statement. Possibly, I should ask a bear.

The second flyer, quotes the park service, in and assures visitors like myself that the people of Seeley Lake "are very accepting and accommodating, respectful of other opinions and preferences." I'm not sure what to make of this statement either. Possibly, I should engage a local resident in a political conversation to test this.

The second sip of coffee clears my head. The bear might be the wiser choice.

But first there is coffee to drink. Even if it's hotel coffee. Once more I dine on a sugary Danish topped with sugary white frosted something, filled with sugary soft something. I toss aside the plastic covering before I'm tempted to read all of the ingredients.

A third brochure, less stressful reading than the label on the food, tells me that Seeley Lake, Montana, lies between two mountain ranges. The Swan Mountains and the Mission Mountains. The Mission range garnered its name due to the relative proximity to the Jesuit Ignatius Mission. The Swan Range achieved its name either in honor of Emmett Swan, a long-time resident of the area or as a natural namesake of nearby Swan Lake. The lake being named after the Swans who used to call it home.

I read further: there are three hundred fifty miles of groomed snow mobile paths for one's winter enjoyment. I'm glad to be here in higher temperatures.

According to the national park service, Seeley Lake lies upstream of a creek named by the Lewis and Clark expedition as Werner Creek. Today it is called the

Clearwater River. The park service also refers to the wildlife here as also "still wild". Where is that bear when I need him?

Mentally ready and fully filled with inflammation inducing Danish treats, I stroll outside. A fully charged battery does its job and I'm off. I don't see any bears. Wild or otherwise. I don't see any welcoming locals, respectful of other opinions or otherwise. I wonder if they would be respectful of the opinions of an invading army of bears?

At first the road is open, well packed and the big Suzuki eats the miles. For two hours I ride at forty miles an hour. Rarely is this possible. Both due to road conditions and to my own fear factor. But so far, I'm flying. I feel the single cylinder torque push me along in more comfort than I thought possible. Tires grip with superb traction. The view ahead is far enough so that I can ride at this quicker pace without fear of danger around a corner. All good things must end.

The road narrows, becomes more uneven, somehow thicker, more of a "watch out or I will bite you" nature. Not severe, just no longer the forty mile per hour gravy train I had been enjoying. The bike and I enter into another section of forest. The shade of the tall trees darkens the road. I remove my sunglasses. An eerie feeling covers my back.

Mind games.

Can't shake this feeling. Rational thought tells me to relax. Yet, every time I enter a stretch of particularly remote geography, my mind says, "Whoa. Get in and get out. Ride easy but make steady time. Don't F this up".

I carry a full set of tools. Plenty of water. Food. Tent. Down sleeping bag. Tire changing equipment. And, for some sense of protection, a GPS tracking device with a pre-paid plan. If I press the button, emergency responders are notified. I am well prepared. With *stuff*. Experience wise, maybe not enough.

Friends and family wrongly believe that because I have previously ridden the Trans-America Trail, Tennessee to Oregon, on dirt, that I am some kind of expert. When I tell them, of poor planning, flat tires, getting lost, getting found, carburetor issues and the like, they just laugh. The truth is, all I know is that if I just ride today, and make a few miles, and that if I ride tomorrow and make a few miles, and if I keep doing that, next thing you know, I'll arrive somewhere. It's more perseverance than aptitude.

It is a mental exercise also. Frame of mind is everything. And mine, today is one of caution. Yesterday was different. I know not why. But today, there is a feeling of "be careful".

I buck up and ride. Still, mind games rule the day.

Several times on this ride, in very remote areas, I've come across someone solo, peddling a mountain bike. Carrying camping gear. They too ride the Continental Divide. The daylight hours available and the massive miles they must cover between towns, ensures that they will camp. Somewhere remote. Me? I twist a throttle to reach a hotel.

The trail, north of Butte, Montana, possibly due to a road closure, and the required reroute, is the most challenging so far on this journey. Both in severity of incline and its loose rock-strewn nature. This heavy Suzuki DR650, loaded with gear should not be willing to climb and dodge and weave and pull like a possessed tractor. But climb and weave it does. *It* is not the weak link.

It's early afternoon when I ride through Helena, Montana. Charming town. If the mural and boutique signs are any indication, Helena is obviously inhabited by women of equal parts intellect and sensibility.

Mural in Helena, Mt.

Lingerie and Romance, Helena, MT.

A sign on a window is further proof that I need to move West. Not only are western women mostly of fine humor, but according to the sign in the window, they are also inclined towards lingerie and romance. Even Shrek knows that lingerie and romance go together like parfait and chocolate.

The day progresses. The weather holds. The trail darts into and out of forests. I unzip all vents in my jacket to welcome the warmth of the afternoon. The summer weight gloves I wear are perfect. This motorcycle does not have heated grips and so far on this ride, they would not have been necessary. I ride with the visor of my helmet raised. The resulting air dries out my eyes, but is nice, nonetheless. I don't wear goggles. Many off road riders enjoy goggles. I've never found a pair that didn't cause my eye glasses to fog.

Even with dry eyes, I can see a mountain biker in the distance, pedaling in the same direction I travel. When I catch up with him, I pull alongside and wave. He motions for me to stop.

"Hey, mind if I get a fix off of your GPS? Mine died yesterday. My name's Fred."

"Not at all," I tilt my Garmin towards him, "How in the heck are you finding your way?" I ask.

"I've got paper maps, but they sure are a pain to use. The scale is huge. I'll replace the GPS once I reach Butte. I've also got maps downloaded on the phone, but they aren't the same as using a GPS."

He jots down the longitude and latitude from my GPS. I wonder how that will help on a map with such large scale. But he seems satisfied.

I almost asked about the maps downloaded onto his phone but caught myself.

Anyone of a certain age will remember the conversation in a movie called "City Slickers" where one of the characters tries to explain to another character how to use a device to record TV shows.

I imagined the map downloading conversation to go about as well. So, I didn't ask. Later, I would play it out in my head.

"So, you download the maps, but can you use them while your cell phone isn't connected to a cell tower, and if so, since your cell phone can't connect, how does it know where you are on the map you downloaded?"

"Well, you see..."

And it goes on for over thirty minutes, until the guy overhearing the conversation, says ...

"Ah, just shut up, please, he's never going to get it. By now, even the cows know how to record a TV show."

I stick to easier conversation, because I'm the guy who is never going to get it, and learned that he too had begun at the Canadian border. He had shipped his bike to Eureka, and through a series of flights and other transport shipped himself there as well. Fred was from Los Angeles, California, was twenty-five years old and slightly jaded about the future of the State.

"I can't afford a house, even with a good job and there is no way I'm staying there much longer. The taxes suck. The traffic sucks. The women wait table and think they are soon to be entitled movie stars. They won't date you unless you have a place on the beach. This trip is my way of beginning to leave. I took the summer off, but probably won't go back to my job. Or maybe more to Northern California. I hear its better there."

Maybe it's my grey hair that had him talking, or maybe he rightly knows that who am I going to tell?

My own opinion on California is less severe. They do have some nice roads.

Fred had no time frame to reach the Mexican border, "I'll get there when I get there. Or I won't. Either way, I can live with it. Maybe I'll meet a nice sensible girl somewhere between Montana and Mexico and settle down."

"Ever been married?" I ask.

"Once," he replies.

"Still want to do it again?"

"It was three years ago; I've forgotten all the pain." He laughs, "Sort of like falling off this mountain bike once a few years back into a cactus. I still have the memory, but the thorns are gone."

"Sounds like neither of us are poster children for long lasting relationships," says I.

"You been married?" he asks.

"I think I'll plead the fifth." I reply.

"Hey, want to swap rides for a hundred miles or so?" Fred smiled.

"I'd hate to ruin your adventure."

"My adventure is hurting my ass today. But tomorrow will be better. It almost always is."

I wish him well and ride on. He is out of sight in my rear-view mirror within thirty seconds. That is a level of commitment I do not possess. Nor does my ass.

Thoughts of peddling and of relationships give me something over which to stir as I make my way towards Butte. The former may be easier than the latter. Each has its uphill struggle and downhill bliss. At least with a long ride on a mountain bike, there is a map. There is also less to negotiate and if a certain section is too rough, one can just get off and walk. Or park it for a month. Or two. Women tend not to want to be parked for a month. Or two.

Jordan Peterson, clinical psychologist and author has written that men and women in relationships are very poor at telling each other what they want and what they need and are even poorer at negotiation in obtaining those wants and needs. He goes on to say that in general, be it in relationship or in daily life, few are comfortable saying what they need, often acting in a manner which almost guarantees they will not get what they want and need. Years of frustration build like steam in a kettle until something has to give. A sad state of affairs. But likely true.

A motorcycle expert, I am not. A relationship expert I am not. I just twist the throttle and see where I end up for the day. Maybe it will be a coffee shop. Maybe they have a mild brew and a sugar free Danish filled with healthy vegetables that taste exactly like vanilla. Maybe my next relationship will be like a downhill bicycle ride or a warm day with a swimming pool at the bottom.

Before me, the route widens. I can see a valley below. A series of extensive curves gradually reduces the altitude. This section is once again hard packed and relaxed riding. I stand on the pegs, not out of necessity from road conditions but out of a need to stretch, and to enjoy the air.

Butte, Montana, tosses out a welcome mat. I dust off my boots and ride on in.

Butte, like many towns of the West, began as a mining town. Copper was the game and European settlers were eager to play. Jobs were available. Something not so easily acquired in sections of Europe at the time. Butte attracted a large number of Irish immigrants to work in the mines. Still today, Butte has the largest percentage of Irish of any city in America, according to Wikipedia. I assume Wikipedia is correct, but I once read in Wikipedia that frogs can fly, so your guess is as good as mine.

I do know that Butte is fifty-five hundred feet above sea level and that as I ride into Butte on this summer day, the altitude makes for some mighty fine weather.

It didn't take long to find a suitable hotel. Next-door was a suitable restaurant. I sat at the bar on a tall seat, one with a cross brace in just the right place for one's feet. The menu offered a variety of burgers. Cow. Elk. Bison and Turkey. The Turkey seemed a bit out of place, this being the West and all.

The nice lady behind the bar approached.

"What can I get for you?" A woman's voice asks.

She was short, maybe five-two. She wore a starched white button-down shirt, unbuttoned at the top revealing just enough of what nature had granted her. And nature had granted her very well. Her jeans were black and of a heavy weight cotton, not the stretchy thin type often seen masquerading as women's jeans. They fit her perfectly. As did the shirt. She was not thin. She had curves. Lots of curves in lots of nice places. She was a living breathing Bob Seger Song.

She bent slightly, using a cloth to wipe the bar in front of me. As she bent, the shirt lowered. She pretended not to notice. I also pretended not to notice. This is a game played out in the bars and restaurants worldwide. Everyone knows the rules. You may look, but if caught looking you must immediately look elsewhere. A blush would be appropriate. For you, not her.

She glanced left, hearing a coworker's voice, as her cloth continued wiping the bar.

I looked but wasn't caught. After looking, I decided then and there, I ain't going back to Georgia.

I felt guilty. For about a second.

The bar now clean, she says, "Sorry, that needed doing."

Me, "Does anyone ever order the turkey burger?"

"I've been here two years. Never sold one." She says, ignoring my faux pas, as I'm sure she had done a million times before.

"I'll take that as a message. OK, let's go with the Bison burger and a side salad." I'm thinking to myself that maybe a salad offsets the Danish for breakfast and the Cliff bar for lunch.

"Good choice." Says she.

"If I had ordered the turkey burger, would you have still said good choice out of politeness."

"I'm polite, but probably not that polite." She gave me a smile.

And with that, she pivots and disappears to the place that bartenders disappear to. I wonder if a woman in possession of her perfect fitting attire knows the secret to relationship negotiation. For a second, I consider asking when she returns. Not in an intrusive way, but in the manner of two strangers just talking. I have no agenda. I'm seriously not interested in a flirtatious conversation. I'm tired, I'm hungry. I'm sleepy. I probably reek of road.

But maybe she is a Jordan Peterson expert.

Not long thereafter, she brings a huge Bison burger.

"It's the best burger in town." She says.

"It looks perfect." I say.

"Sorry it took so long; we don't get many requests for a side salad. You must be passing through. But I do like the blue pants."

"They were a gift."

"You should have given them back at Christmas." And with the words I was treated to a sideways head nod and one raised eyebrow.

"I wore them in honor of the state flower."

"No way the state flower is that color blue. I'm from Oregon originally, so I don't know about the Montana State flower. Is it really blue?"

"Sort of purple, from what I read." But it's close.

"You should still give them back for Christmas. Or maybe just donate them. Oh, wait, they must be motorcycle pants. We get a lot of motorcycle riders through here."

"Yep, they are. I'm one of those bikers."

"Sounds like fun. A lot of the guys bring their map in here, the owner knows a lot of trails around here. You looking for a trail?"

"No, I'm just looking for someone who knows Jordan Peterson." I couldn't help myself.

She hesitated. Her eyes looked upwards and to the left. Then the nod and grin of recognition. "I know Jordan, he's that old cowboy, lives down on West Granite Street. Enjoy your burger." And she was off.

Oh well.

Back at the hotel, I find blazing speeds for their internet. I've never seen such fast page downloads, not at Starbucks, not at McDonald's, not nowhere.

The speed allows for surfing in the extreme. I read of Nez Perce, early American explorers, fierce battles between various Indian tribes and those explorers. It all seems to run together; one dismemberment, torture and other equally disturbing event after another. I am reminded of the old newspaper adage, "if it bleeds, it leads."

I guess the internet is no different, each webpage trying to out gore the others to attract visitors. I'm tired of reading about blood and guts along the Continental Divide.

Surely, there is more alluring history.

Then I see it.

The year was 1806.

A Nez Perce boy was born.

He grew like other Nez Perce children, learning the customs and manner of his people. But this boy was different. He had always been so.

From the exact moment of his birth, he came into the world with different characteristics from the other children.

History does not tell us if he was treated with antithetic propriety. In fact, until the 1870's history tells us nothing of him at all. But there are clues, uncomfortable clues.

Then the boy, now a man, met William H. Jackson. Jackson was a photographer known for his western images and traveled to the area of the Continental Divide in an effort to document the landmarks of the west.

His equipment was heavy. They large cameras used glass plates. On one trip, one of the normally surefooted mules carrying the equipment tripped. A month's worth of images was damaged. Jackson made the journey again, capturing some of his most well-known images. His notoriety made him well known to the Indians.

On one photography trip, an elderly Nez Perce approached him. The boy, always different than the others was now old. His hair was blonde. His features both Indian and European.

He spoke to Jackson.

"I am the son of William Clark."

Of Lewis and Clark fame.

Day 4

Butte, Montana to Lima, Montana

Today, I will learn that some history, the Native American lingerie kind never made it into high school history books.

I awake in a fairly comfortable bed. I notice that I'm still breathing. All my parts appear to be working. I feel like how I imagine that old cowboy would feel. Worn in some places. Worn out in others.

I recall the mountain biker from the day before.

Those are people I admire. Most were not born with the infinite athletic ability. Fewer still are wealthy trust funders with time on their hands that they are trying to fill. They simply want to fulfill a dream and along the way in a life that can sometimes have a few clouds to find life's silver lining.

My own clouds have been few on this ride. I could go so far to say that the entire ride has been silver. No lining needed.

I stroll down to the small breakfast room where I am greeted with hotel hot coffee and hope. A hope that words written the night before, on social media, describing the days ride, have been noticed. In a few moments, I will learn. Yes. Or no.

The extravagant middle priced hotel has a breakfast area where high carbohydrate, low health offerings keep the coffee company. Its unfortunate coffee so perhaps it deserves unfortunate food friends. Looking around the breakfast area I notice the average waist line is as unfortunate as the food. Reasoning that I will work hard today, sitting on a motorcycle seat, I dig in.

Then I fire up the iPad and check social media for a "like". I suspected a certain unobtainable someone was following this ride.

A photo I had posted had one particular "like." And it was, like, well, you know, like it was the "like" I was hoping for. I would have tossed my hair, but it's too short.

There were miles to make. Photos to take. Dust to raise. Because of and in spite of the artery clogging breakfast, I was hungry for more.

Anyone who has sampled an hors d'oeuvre of America's scenery along remote roads are likely to be soon fueled with an appetite for the entire seven course meal. A meal consumed along the pathways constructed and traveled long ago by those carrying black powder dreams of land, and freedom and their own restless future.

The final course, a desert, be it a double scoop of Cookies and Cream or the finish line of a long ride, beckons like a scantily clad unobtainable model at a motorcycle show. Except, finishing the Continental Ride is actually obtainable. And costs far less in the long run.

My own unobtainable model, Samantha was her name, was reading my internet posts. She lingered in my rear-view mirror. I had left her there several months earlier when we had met and had become friends. We remained only friends and I was convinced we should remain only friends.

I had ridden away, but I hadn't actually left. Her image haunted me as surely as the words beneath the waters in Norman McClean's *"A River Runs Through It"* haunted its narrator as he recalled those in his life who are now gone.

Instead of being too expensive to obtain, she was proving to be too expensive to ignore and money had nothing to do with the equation.

Her life was in Arizona, far from my own, completely different, both in life's geography and in life's experiences. I wrote not just to share my Continental Divide experience but, in the hope, she would read the most important of meanings, those between the lines.

For a second, I ask myself if a "like" could also be read between its lines.

Onward, towards courteous gravel roads, wide, well kept, out of sight of the main travel route, out of the way and simply outstanding.

The route from Butte, Montana two hundred miles southward is a dual sport riders' best friend.

Forgiving of your faults and encouraging you to forge ahead, ready to be there by your side the whole way.

The Suzuki is doing a superb job. It climbs when I ask it to climb. It cruises at 40 mph when needed. It cruises on pavement at 60 when needed.

The seat, made by that long time maker of motorcycle seats "Corbin", is comfortable.

The handlebars, their width and their height fit me well.

My notes of this day speak only of easy miles where one can relax. No sand lies in the path ready to scare the heck out of you. No off camber blind corners. Nothing of consequence other than easy mile after easy mile. Riding a dual sport motorcycle on days like this feels like being inside a poster hanging on a motorcycle dealer show room floor.

The sun is out, but it's not too hot. The skyline is attainable. You often stand on the foot pegs, with visor open, taking in the exactness of crisp air passing through the vents in your jacket, through your helmet, along the outside of your legs and you feel as if you are a part of it all. The moment seems to last longer than normal. You lose all track of time as another vista reveals itself taking your eyes further down the road, knowing it can't last, but it does. You ride on. On these days, darkness will come too soon.

Then you remember. In locations like this one, it's the hour before darkness that holds some of the utmost beauty, the grandest of light and some of the greatest of threats. Wildness appears in that light. Some of it harmless, too small to threaten. Others, like deer, antelope and elk are the reason. The reason to slow the pace. To make camp or find a hotel.

Towards the end of this day in its own grand light, I pause to take a photo.

As darkness overcomes the day, I am fortunate to find a room in what appears to be the only hotel in town. Just down the street, I find a restaurant, where I treat myself to a very cold beer, open the computer and do my best to describe the day.

It had been a day defined once more by easy gravel, allowing good speed and good time to be made. A pair of new Kenda dual sport tires, installed before leaving Ridgway, has served me well. Fairly inexpensive, decent on pavement and while not as well suited to dirt as something like a Dunlop 606, they did the dirt job just fine.

I'm not a tire guy. Give me whatever is available, and I'll work with it. The likely reason, I'm not a tire guy, is that I don't ride hard enough to know the difference. I don't ride fast enough on pavement to know much difference there either. Don't get me wrong, I can tell a crappy weaving large knobby on pavement from a good road tire, but all in all, I don't get too worked up about it. I'm not in a hurry.

Before leaving Ridgway, I had attended to the service needs of the DR650, changing the oil, draining and refilling the brake fluid, installing a new chain and inspecting the front and rear sprocket, which were in good shape. Tightening a bolt here, a screw there and in general performing a front to back close inspection. So far, so good.

My previous unprepared ride on the Trans-America Trail had taught me the lesson of homework.

Before retiring for the evening, I retreat once more to the internet to the history of this area.

The year was 1805.

Men who made their way west were about to learn that native women had more on their mind than cooking.

But first.

Born to Nez Perce parents Tuekakas and Khapkhaponimi, a young boy named Hallalhotsoot, watched his elders greet an exhausted group of travelers. His father later became known as Chief Twisted Hair.

Though he was young, born just eight years earlier in 1797, Hallalhotsoot knew much of the habits and customs of his people. He knew well how to ride a horse, his tribe one of the earliest adopters of horsemanship. His manner was forthright. He knew his place and did not interfere with the elders. He listened. He watched. He noticed the way the elders interacted.

Their caution as well as their curiosity. The boy didn't know it then, but he was about to play a role in one of recent histories most storied encounters.

The weary travelers were none other than Lewis and Clark. The meeting took place within four hundred miles of this hotel, on the western side of the Continental Divide.

The boy would later become known as Chief Lawyer, for his negotiating skills in dealing with the white man and would become a role model for the male definitions of behavior and social norms of his tribe. He would fight the enemies known as Shoshone, Northern Paiute and the ever-expanding settlers from the East. His reputation was rightly earned through both battle and forced compromise, equal choices of fate, the times and the tribe unto which he was born and his adherence to what it means to be a man in his tribal world view.

The young boy and the Nez Perce lived along the game trails and rivers that today make up the western boundaries of the Continental Divide.

As I read of Hallalhotsoot, and of Lewis and Clark, the obvious comfort of my own travel so close to where they met is in stark contrast not only in the ease of roads on which to make substantial time, but also in the circumstances to which men of my day were born, unweighted by such severity of compromise and unaired in navigating hundreds of miles mostly upstream and over mountain ranges in search of a trade passage to the Pacific. In search of greater commerce.

Along the way, they hunted for food, adopted to surroundings and chose a place to camp for the night. No cheap burger on the menu. No hotel in sight.

The Nes Pearce mostly lived between Latitude lines 45 North to Latitude 47 North.

It was into this territory that Lewis and Clark had come. They had walked up over and through what is known as Lo Lo Pass, traveling east to west, crossing the Bitterroot Mountain range and suffering greatly in the process.

It was late September as the men finally made their way down the pass, where they came into one of the villages of the Nez Perce tribe. Chief Twisted Hair greeted the group. The travelers appeared tired, hungry, haggard, exhausted and somewhat lost.

Chief Twisted Hair sat with the men and through a frustrating time of making signs appeared to reach an understanding of what the men sought.

Twisted Hair and the men of his tribe, sometimes, made their own way through Lo Lo pass, to hunt the buffalo that inhabited the plains east of the Bitter Root Mountains. They knew all too well the hazards and endurance the trip entailed. At this point in time, the Nez Perce were not well equipped in fire arms and were eager to trade for them, which would make their own survival hunting for Buffalo and other game far easier.

Guns would also make them less vulnerable to their enemies. Into this situation entered the Corps of Discovery, the special unit of the young United States Army led by Lewis and Clark.

It is unclear if Lewis actually traded guns for horses with Chief Twisted Hair. Lewis's account, in his journal speaks of trading camphor to be used on the sore back of chief's wife. He also mentions dispensing "eye wash". These two items were said to be traded for two horses. Some historians believe it is more likely was the alluded promise of a new trade route, promising guns and other real benefits which enticed the Chief to help.

History writers, in an attempt to overstate the benefit of the "medical" assistance provided by Lewis and Clark, described such help as frequently treating the illnesses and diseases of the Nez Perce. This was a time of no aspirin, no antibiotics, no anti-bacterial ointment, and very little actual medical assistance would have been possible. But medical assistance, like beauty, is in the eye of the beholder.

The Nez Perce had gained a reputation for breeding horses. Lewis's journal describes the horses as "excellent race, they are lofty, elegantly formed, active and durable, in short, many of them look like the fine English horses. "

Tribes of the West had acquired horses left behind by the Spanish in about the 1730's. By the time Lewis wrote in his journal, tribes had experimented for seventy years with breeding techniques.

The now famous Nez Perce Chief Joseph, who would, in 1877, so proudly fight, on horseback, the final intrusions into his land would not be born for forty more years. At the time of Lewis and Clark's expedition, the entire population of the United States was five and a half million.

After Lewis and Clark, trappers came west. But they came in small numbers. These numbers did not represent a threat to the Nez Perce or any other tribes of the west.

Before Lewis and Clark, there were French and Spanish explorers periodically in the area, but they were also few in number.

In 1805, Chief Twisted Hair, not only didn't see Lewis and Clark as a huge threat, but he saw them as a potential benefit. Reports mention that he was reasonably cautious at first meeting, but warmed to the idea of beneficial trade.

The Nez Perce lived in upwards of one hundred Nez Perce villages in an area of seventeen million acres in what is now Oregon, Idaho, Montana and

Washington. Population, depending on which historian is to be believed reached four to six thousand souls.

Had Twisted Hair known what was to come seventy years later, he likely would not have traded so easily with the expedition or at least would have warned his son to always be wary of men from the east.

Lewis and Clark were to remain several days with the Nez Perce who assisted them in finding wood to build canoes and trading with them for fresh horses.

While reading historical accounts of Lewis and Clark and of their encounters with the native population, one awkward report couldn't help but be noticed.

It seems that many natives believed that spiritual strength could be passed through shall we say "relations" with those deemed to possess the strength. The natives saw the guns and other artifacts of the expedition as strength. Hence the women of the tribe were very friendly to the expedition.

In Clarks own words. "An old woman and wife to a chief of the Chinooks came and made a camp near ours. She brought with her six young squaws. I believe for the purpose of gratifying the passions of the men of our party. "

Another Tribe, the Shoshones appeared to become resentful if their women were rejected.

In the Pacific Northwest, the Clatsop and Chinook used sex for trade, to the point where Lewis warned his men against running out of provisions.

If the old blonde Indian who confessed his lineage to a photographer is to be believed, Lewis should have given the same warning to Clark.

As I read, I am curious about my own ride into this territory and what adventure it might bring.

Eager to learn the lessons of trade with locals taught by the Corps of Discovery, I check my provisions. I find them lacking. Oh well.

There is trade for "services" and there is trade for goods. Those who came before and after Lewis and Clark came to trade goods, even so many of the mountain men for traders took Indian wives.

The Spanish, French and American men who once roamed these lands engaging in trade wore felt hats, leather ornaments, linen hunting frocks and often used a long flintlock smoothbore to hunt their meals. The guns had special appeal to the natives.

These diverse guns were capable of being loaded with fine pellets for bird hunting or a lethal sixty caliber round ball for larger game. The inside bore of the long barrel of these guns was not rifled. It was smooth, from which they got their name. Smooth bore. Rifling would have provided greater accuracy, but long-range accuracy was not necessary in thick forest or when propelling tiny shot upwards to secure a duck for dinner.

Smooth bores are a challenge to shoot well, especially when ignited by flint. Much can go wrong. Dampness can affect the black powder in the resulting in a poof, but no bang. Not the end of one's day when sighting in a bird. Quite possibly the end of one's day and the end of one's future when faced with a wary bear or a warring enemy.

Gun technology of the day was primitive compared to modern weapons. Even so, it was far superior to using a bow and arrow or throwing a spear. The tribes of the West were rightly impressed with the weaponry of Lewis and Clark and of all the trappers and traders they met.

Those bold souls who used these guns needed to carry the accoutrements necessary to make them function. So, hung from their shoulder, they carried a cow's horn, capped on one end and plugged with pointed wood or leather on the other, holding within its confines, black powder. Powder they were careful to keep dry.

Wet powder would not fire. Wet powder hunters would not eat that day.

In addition, a leather bag, called a "possibles bag", worn on a leather belt, or also hung from their shoulder held sixty caliber round lead balls, fine lead or steel pellets and spare flints necessary to provide the spark to ignite a small amount of black powder placed in a shallow pan.

The sixty caliber is a reference to the ball having a diameter of point six of an inch, a little more than half an inch. Not something anyone welcomes being struck by after being fired from the end of one of these guns. It is a huge mass of lead.

According to "*RendezvousCountry.com*", asking a mountain man about his personal items, he would have said, "these are my possibles". The bag has also been called a long hunter bag or a muzzle loader pouch.

Pulling the trigger on one of these guns, after loading it with contents of the possibles bag, levered an arm, via a spring. Not a spring in the sense of being wound, like a coil, rather it is a piece of folded over steel, like a V shape. The open end of the V, when held compressed, then quickly released, provides a spring back effect.

This arm being levered is called a hammer, and it has jaws, squeezed together by a long screw, between the jaws, was a piece of flint, a quartz material that creates a spark when struck against steel. To insert a new flint, the screw was turned counterclockwise, thus opening the jaws. Insert new flint. Tighten the screw.

The flint was held in place also by a small piece of leather to prevent it from cracking by the force of tightening the jaws.

A flintlock uses two piles of black powder, a mixture of Sulphur, charcoal and saltpeter. Also called gun powder. One pile is poured down the barrel of the gun. The other, much smaller pile is placed in what is called the pan, of the flintlock mechanism.

Over the years, gun owners learn to measure the amount of powder poured into the barrel and the amount of powder placed in the pan.

The pan is simply a small bowl-shaped recess. Snuggled up next to the pan, is a tiny hole that was drilled through the gun barrel, so that it aligns exactly opposite the pile of black powder that was poured down the barrel.

A larger diameter barrel may require a different amount of powder than one of smaller diameter. A one-hundred-yard shot may require a different amount of powder than a twenty-yard shot.

Like the spread sheets of today, men's nature calculated the best through trial and error, writing down the results, fine tuning for their particular gun.

With the knowledge of powder to be used, the hunter is ready.

The hunter spots game. He has already poured black powder down his barrel. Over the black powder, he placed a small patch of cotton. Over this piece of cotton, he rammed a round lead ball, or lots of tiny pieces of pellets. He has also pre-loaded the pan of his flintlock mechanism.

There might be difficulties in his weapon of choice, but unlike the boy crouched behind a rock, there is no need to fear a tiniest of branch wreaking havoc with his dinner plans.

He pulls back the hammer. It clicks into place, held there by a notch in the trigger mechanism. Pulling back the hammer has, along with it, held in its jaws, pulled back the piece of sharp flint.

He aims. He pulls the trigger, releasing the hammer from its notch, thus propelling the flint towards the frizzen. The flint strikes the metal frizzen, and if all goes according to plan, the flint striking the metal frizzen produces a spark. The spark ignites the small pile of black powder in the pan.

The spark travels into and through the tiny hole in the gun barrel, called the touch hole, where that spark ignites the black powder that was measured and then poured down the barrel. This powder is referred to as the main charge. If this main charge ignites, an explosion occurs. There is nowhere for this energy to go but out through the barrel, propelling the round lead ball, or tiny shot, outwards, towards the target.

If the main charge is wet there will be no explosion. Or if the gun maker drilled the hole in a manner that didn't place it exactly opposite of the main charge, there will be sometimes be no explosion. The result is known as a flash in the pan, meaning only the small pile of black powder in the pan ignites, but not the primary charge.

Other factors can ruin the sequence. If the hunter didn't clean the touch hole after a few shots, it may clog with black powder residue, and no explosion. If the hunter got in a hurry and mistakenly placed the lead ball down the barrel then in a backwards sequel, on top of it, poured the powder, no explosion. Or he forgot to pour any powder at all into the barrel, only loading the lead ball, no explosion. This last example is called "dry balling". It happens, way more than you would expect. I've done it more than once.

For all of these reasons and more, gun technology advanced. Flint locks for combat and for most hunting are ancient history. Like the bow and arrow and the spear.

To further complicate the matter, each hunter had to learn his gun. Some guns performed better with a certain amount of powder, not too much, not too little.

The amount of powder used can and does affect the accuracy. As mentioned, at one hundred yards, the same gun will shoot high or low, depending on the amount of black powder used in the barrel. Hunters carried a small measuring device, usually brass, because brass does not spark.

Later "mountain men" carried more reliable Hawken rifles, manufactured by Jacob and Samuel Hawken in St. Louis, Missouri. The brothers set up shop in 1815. Their gun was lighter weight than the long-barreled predecessors. Many used a percussion lock, rather than a flint lock. A small premade cap, like a tiny thimble, was far more reliable than flint and frizzen.

This cap was manufactured with powder inside. It is hollow. The cavity, as mentioned is filled with black powder. The open end of this tiny thimble fits over a small tit on the new and improved percussion mechanism on the side of the gun. Ignition is more reliable. Less prone to operator error. The hunter still had to properly load the barrel with the prime load of black powder and a patch and a lead ball. So, human error was still possible.

Writing this book, in a condo in Arizona, I too have a historical connection with the early days of black powder hunting.

On a wall in my den hangs a small caliber rifle. My grandfather purchased this from a gun maker. It was not mass produced. It was hand produced.

Its use was likely small game for the dinner table. I'm not usually one to retain artifacts from my family's past. I keep only two items. A porcelain liquor label, owned by my grandmother who hung it over decanters in a time of more refinement than my current life, and this old, rusted cap lock rifle, with its possible bag and powder horn.

Later gunsmiths understood that removing the chance of wet powder was needed, so later improvements resulted in the cartridge we know today. A sealed brass cartridge, with the gun powder inside, protected from the elements and from the error of humans.

The barrels on these guns were rifled which puts a spin onto the lead projectile making it far more accurate than a smooth bore. If one was to place a light and look down into one of these barrels one would see a twist cut into the steel, like a candy cane.

This twist grabbed the lead ball, spinning it as it made its way out the barrel after have been exploded outward by the ignition of the prime charge. The lead ball is grabbed by the rifling twist because each barrel had an opening designed to be used with a particular sized round ball.

For baseball fans out there, think of a knuckleball and how it tumbles. Then think of a fast ball, spinning and how it flies. If a pitcher could spin the baseball exactly like the rifling of a bore, the ball would travel fairly straight, mostly unaffected by gravity, but not tumbling like a knuckle ball. Smooth bore guns were prone to sending the round ball tumbling, which produced accuracy only to a short distance, seventy yards or so.

Sparks provide the flame that propels an object towards the goal. Be it flint on frizzen, or a long-distance motorcycle rider, a spark is necessary. The men who traveled westward did not do so fueled solely by curiosity. Commerce was the main spark.

Columbus didn't sail westward for the joy of ocean travel. He sailed westward for commerce, gold, silver and other trade goods. Likewise, Americans didn't travel into the westward reaches for the joy of travel by land or by river. They sought the commerce of the day. All of the attire and flints and powder were simply the tools to attain the commerce.

Customers in both the New England colonies and Europe paid exorbitant prices for fur. Natives were all too happy to engage in this trade, swapping the metal knives and later the guns of the Americans for the furs at which they had long been expert in obtaining.

Each party satisfying a commercial need in the process. Some things never change. Beaver, in particular was popular. Two thirds of all hats in Europe, in the early 1800's was made of Beaver.

Much of Europe is prone to rain and snow. Beaver held its shape in such conditions and was moisture resistant. No wonder Beaver were almost hunted to extinction. Fashion and function were gradually replaced by synthetic material.

Today's dual sport riding Johnny-comes-lately explorers don't don themselves in linen and leather and fur. Instead, they wear waterproof textile and waterproof riding boots. Around their mid sections, instead of a possibles bag, many wears twelve-volt heated vests plugged directly into another of man's marvels, the battery. Meals are taken either by boiling water in a small camp stove and adding freeze dried meals or at a small-town diner. No black powder required.

Do I scoff at such apparel or the manner in which we travel on two comfortable wheels? Not at all. Even Lewis and Clark would have happily worn modern clothing and would have preferred a more comfortable means of reaching the sands of the Pacific.

Day 5

Lima, Montana to Jackson, Wyoming

Today, I will meet a man who walked over six million steps, one stride at a time towards a goal few obtain.

I awake, in Lima, Montana, to the smell of coffee.

In my stupor, I imagine a medium brew, with mellow traits and cold Irish Cream sitting nearby, ready to transform the slight bitterness into a sweetness laced with slight decadence. I imagine a thin, aptly endowed brunette full of life and wearing dangling jewelry and a tight T-shirt. I see her serving the coffee in a hand turned mug, gentle steam rising like my hopes and dreams.

Then I fully awaken. Bummer.

As I wake, I realize there is no barista in this room. There isn't even a coffee maker in this room. There isn't even a high carb breakfast bar in the lobby. But I smell coffee.

Scratching my head and my eyes, determined to remain asleep I turn over and find the cell phone on the night stand.

The clock on its face reads 7:30. Knowing that nothing worthwhile ever happens before 10am, I roll over.

Then, there it is again. Coffee.

Arghhh........Moan. Whine. I'm now awake because my imagination has a caffeine addition.

Then, I see movement. Draperies are blowing in a gentle wind. I'd left the window open. The aroma is coming from outside. Gathering a towel for modesty, I walk towards the window and peek out. Someone had left a large metal travel mug, it's top removed, sitting on the low-lying railing. Hot mist rose from it and blew towards me like an invitation. No one was in sight.

I was tempted.

I had one of those moments of internal conversation.

"Naw, wouldn't be right."

"Take it as a good omen. The Roman coffee Gods are looking out for you."

"I'm sleepy and really want some coffee, but right is right. Besides, whoever left it there is missing their expensive stainless-steel mug. Take it down to the lobby as a lost and found."

"Good plan. On the way to the lobby, you could take a few sips. It's a win-win."

"Do what you will, but you look damn silly standing here in a short white hotel towel drooling over a cup of coffee. "

I have no idea if the owner returned for their mug. More likely the hotel clerk has themselves a nice stainless coffee mug. I confess to sniffing the steam as I took it to the front desk.

Virtue may be its own reward, but I still had to go through the six steps to ride to breakfast. Along the way, I didn't see a single Roman God of coffee, or a blonde. Sure was a nice mug though.

There is a small restaurant just down the road. An older gentleman was behind the cash register. He sees my helmet.

"What Harley do you ride?" He asks.

"The one made by Suzuki." I say.

"Wouldn't catch me dead on one of them Jap bikes." He says.

He was probably in his late seventies with a roundness of body that I was sure hid a firmness of resolve. I wanted food not an argument. He likely knew more about the finer points of Milwaukee iron than I could ever guess. I thought for a second.

"If Harley made a dirt bike, I'd have bought it."

That seemed to satisfy him.

"Take that first booth on the left. You can hang your jacket up here if you want." I saw his gaze linger for a moment longer than normal on the blue color, the textile material, it not being Harley approved black leather or a vest full of patches. I saw the questions form in his mind seeking to understand why anyone would ride a motorcycle in such garb. He was too polite to ask.

As I walked to the booth, I wondered what roads he had ridden and what stories he could tell. I also wondered if any of those roads had been paved by machinery manufactured outside of Milwaukee.

I understood his mindset. At a certain age, we become weary of things that don't work, or don't fit our world image. Lately I've become weary of cheap Chinese nuts and bolts that strip after one use. I've become weary of those who speak loudly about things of which they know little, hoping volume will make up for lack of knowledge, eager to push their parroted ill-informed point of view on everyone who is unfortunate enough to cross their path.

A law professor of mine referred to such pontificating as gas station law. When men gathered in public places, sometimes at the local gas station, discussing the events of the day, politics, policy, corporate largess or gamesmanship, personal largess or gamesmanship, domestic relations, foreign relations and all the honest or ill-advised means known to mankind. There will always be one or two who are louder than the rest. Uttering such gems as, "That's against the law" or "He ought to be arrested for that."

Say it loud enough and most within earshot will simply stand down, either out of politeness or withdrawal.

Paint a loud negative picture and many listeners, without thinking the thing through for themselves will parrot the speaker that night over the dinner table, it never occurring to them to do a bit of research on the issue, thus passing down the massive load of bull shite to their children.

And so, it goes. Gas station law.

There are well over 3,000 federal criminal statutes. There are another 1000 state criminal statutes. Per state. We have enough "laws" without inventing more at the gas station.

In an attempt to count the total number of federal criminal laws, in 1982, a group was led by Ronald Gaines. After two years, they gave up. Covering twenty-three thousand pages of federal law, Mr. Gaines recognized the task as fruitless.

Consider this the next time you hear of a federal prosecutor searching for crime under which to charge a political opponent. That prosecutor has over 3,000 from which to choose. A state prosecutor likewise has at least an additional 1000 from which to choose.

If a federal or state prosecutor wants to charge someone, because they don't like them, or because they want to disable a political opponent, or bankrupt him or her with legal fees, it's very easy to find a statute that they likely have violated.

Don't believe me? Mind if I take a look at the last 10 years of your tax returns? Is every line; every deduction; every business lunch; every charitable donation of clothes properly valued?

If not, you've just committed tax fraud.

Ever get a mortgage? Did you slightly exaggerate the value of your assets? You just committed mortgage fraud. Ever do any work on your home without a permit?

At a certain age, it's harder to go with the flow, especially when life experience has proven that the flow being sold is not a flow at all, but a mindless float down a river which history has proven to be fraught with rapids, over rocks designed to destroy personal freedom, personal responsibility and personal achievement.

When news is merely the repetition of a "talking point", then there is actually no news at all. On either side of the issue. Ask yourself why these talking points are used and you might not like the answer. They are used because they work.

Calling legislation "the Affordable Care Act", when it is neither affordable nor about care, works because who has time to research it? Even a well-known Senator once said, "we have to pass it to find out what is in it." With leaders like that, who needs enemies?

Politicians routinely enact a 4000-page law without ever reading it. Buried within those pages that you will not read, is plenty of pork to those who support their reelection campaign.

An acquaintance of mine, Scooter Tramp Scotty, whose book "Josie's Journey" is a wild ride through time, said once, "You know, getting older is like watching the same movie, over and over. "

Yea, and the same talking points.

Maybe we learn something after seeing the movie for the fifth time.

Somewhere along the flow, there will come the day when sitting aside your dusty dirt bike, high in the mountains, along a clear creek, you will see, but not hear, a motorcycles approach. An electric Harley Davidson will pull alongside the stream with parts made who knows where, some of which will likely strip after one use.

Time marches on. Sometimes on twelve volts.

I order a pot of coffee and oatmeal with raisons and strawberries. After yesterday's breakfast I'm feeling guilty. I also know that drinking the entire pot of coffee will be a mistake. I do it anyway, blaming it on open windows and the Romans.

In about an hour, in direct relation to the size of this coffee pot, I'm going to need to execute series of pull overs. Preferably close to a large tree. But an hour is forever into the future when sleep is in the eyes.

I lighten the coffee with faux cream from tiny plastic cups, with even tinier thin plastic covers that are nearly impossible to remove with adult sized fingers.

For a moment I contemplate what the day will hold. I have expectations, but know better.

Travel on two wheels is like riding into a magician's act. Just when you think you know where you're going, the path you have chosen offers up a surprise. Like life. Only with less grey hair.

I've ridden my share of long rides. There have been surprises. My hair hasn't been one of them. It's still grey.

To say Lima is rural is an understatement. Population two hundred and twelve. Originally founded as a service center for the Union Pacific Rail Road, it was once named Allerdice. Somewhere along the way, an early settler, from Lima, Ohio had his way and changed the town name.

Wouldn't you just love to know how that went down. I envision a town hall meeting. There are maybe four people in attendance. All town leaders. All eager to get on with their day.

"Any old news?" none heard.

"Any new news?"

A guy in the back raises his hand, "I hereby make a motion to change the name of this town."

"OK, why would we do that?"

"Well, I'm from Lima, Ohio and it's a nice place with nice people. I think this town should also be known as a nice place with nice people."

"Ah, OK, but we already have a name, this is Allerdice."

"Yea, but we all know that the Allerdice name came from the Railroad days and that I've heard that Allerdice wasn't a nice person. And everyone knows he colluded with Russia."

"I didn't know that."

"Furthermore, I just received a talking point from Washington saying that if I tell you that ten times, you start to believe it. And we can call this meeting the Affordable Lima, Montana, Meeting. People will love it."

There is a moment of silence. A gavel is raised and struck.

"Motion passed. Draw it up, but I'm not going to read it."

These days, Lima is full of two hundred twelve nice people. All of those nice people attract mostly other nice people, many of them peddling or walking or motorcycling the Continental Divide. Many, like myself stay at the Mountain View Motel. I wonder what Mr. Allerdice would think of this. If indeed a Mr. Allerdice ever existed.

The oatmeal is gone and the pot empty, I make my way to the register to pay.

The gentleman asks, "Everything ok?"

"Perfect, you guys make a great bowl of oatmeal."

"Thanks. We buy the strawberries local." He adds.

"It was delicious."

"Where you riding today?" He asks.

"I try not to have a definite destination each day. I'm just riding the Continental Divide."

"Well, I'll be danged. A lot of our customers pedal that route. They all got legs like tree trunks."

"Those folks have more dedication than me. I just sit there and turn the throttle. " I say.

His manner has softened. Commonality will do that.

"Well, keep the shiny side up and thanks for coming in."

And I know he meant it. He was genuinely grateful for his customers and paid attention to the details. The place was spotless. The oatmeal was fabulous. His affinity for Harley is born of life experience.

My own Harley Davidson is as old in motorcycle years as that man. It's been around the block enough times to have an opinion and doesn't really care what you think about that opinion. Ride it or don't ride it. Cuss it or love it. Bemoan the shortcomings like uneducated southern humor. It has a pedigree and a rugged tractor like sophistication. It gets the job done.

Most of its parts are metal. Its heavy. The carburetor is Japanese, though it is stamped with the Harley logo. Most of the other parts are pure, made in the USA. For better or for worse.

When I first purchased this seven-hundred-pound beast, I did so mostly out of curiosity, never having owned a Harley of any vintage. After living with it for a year, and becoming more familiar than I had intended with its inner workings, inner primary, outer primary, belt drive, leaking quad seal, one-hundred-and-fifty-foot-pounds torque specification for the compensator nut and all of the other idiosyncrasies of getting to know any motorcycle, it's grown on me. So much so, that I'm looking for a large touring Harley of the same vintage. Go figure.

Back to our story.......dirt roads, a motorcycle named Marilyn and the hope to make it all the way to the Mexican border.

Exiting the café and walking to the DR650, I realize that I haven't' fallen off this Suzuki yet. My ego is intact. Mostly. I did drop it yesterday while dismounting at a lunch stop, failing to notice the uneven ground. No one was around to witness. Maybe that doesn't count as a drop. If a motorcycle falls in the forest and no one hears, did it really fall?

Miles to make. Words that will need to be written. One's mind has a mind of its own. And mine at the moment is on a certain woman in Arizona. Why did I leave Arizona you may ask?

Well, it's complicated. In a simple sort of way. It has to do with age. Mine. And hers.

Before I hop aboard, I take a photo of the bike, using the camera in my cell phone. I have a far better camera in a bag on the gas tank. I have yet to use it. Preferring instead the simplicity of using my cell phone camera, easily reached in the left breast pocket of my jacket.

The motorcycle world, like cell phones, has exploded. Men and women riding long distances on two wheels. What men like Ted Simon and Helge Pederson started, has today become an abbreviation. RTW or

Round the world. There are preferred routes. Preferred seasons. All, I believe, an embrace for change and challenge. Riding towards a circular destination.

Balancing golden dreams on one side of a child's playground teeter totter against being a responsible adult is not an easy task. A RTW rider may not face the same danger as early mountain men but the commitment is the same.

My own tiny commitment today is to just make some miles. Those miles on this day come in a stress-free laidback manner. The trail is wide, sweeping, hard packed. Somewhere during the day, I stop to take yet another photo. With my cell phone.

The old Bannack Road lies in the Beaverhead mountains. It runs between eastern Idaho and Montana. According to Tony Huegel's "Backcountry Byways LLC", over a hundred years ago, it connected the territorial capital of Montana with the small town of

Corinne, Utah and ran near the Continental Railroad. No matter its origins, it is one of the most memorable sections of my ride so far.

The route steadies on. Another day of approaching two hundred miles. Miles easily made due to near perfect conditions. No ruts. No soft dirt. No thick gravel. Roads packed from a fair amount of what I guess to be ranch and farm travel.

Somewhere during the day, I paused for the hope of a quick lunch and some fuel. Coffee, not petrol. I don't remember where or when. There was no charming host or no curious lad to seal the memory. It was small. It was limited in menu. It was closed. But it was well named.

Less than fifty miles outside Whitefish, I pull over for another cup of coffee. I don't need it. I don't really even want it. What I want is to use the cell phone to call Samantha. Holding the phone, I scroll through the numbers until I see hers. I am reminded of sitting near a riding arena guitar in hand, the fingers of my left hand pressing through an A minor scale as I watch her teach a young girl how to saddle the horse. Her voice glides across the Arizona afternoon as the sun, low in the sky clasps her brown hair in its radiance, making it shine.

I decide not to make the call. Maybe another day. But I know, I won't call. There is simply too large of a hurdle between she and I. Besides, I have miles to make. Wheels to turn.

Still, I can hear her voice.

Other than calls I do not make, today presented no severe challenges. I sat most of the day, standing only to stretch my legs. Parts of the day were remote. Others less so. My mind wandered. I sang songs. I wrote songs. I tried to remember the chord progression to "Brown Eyed Girl". I tried to remember the opening lick. My left hand inadvertently making chord shapes against the hand grip. My right foot tapping the beat.

And then.......

The musical moment was interrupted by four Antelope running parallel with Marilyn and I, crazy fast, having been startled by what they must think is a loud Centaur trailing dust.

Why do they run parallel? Why not just veer left? Is it a race? Is it play? Like the porpoise I used to see surfing the bow wave of my sailboat in the Bahamas so many years ago. Are they fearful? Or are they laughing at my straight line when they can veer as easily as kite in the breeze?

Eventually they either tire of the game or just tire, indeed veering left. I am left to my Brown Eyed Girl.

The GPS track is not in tune with my music. Its track is blue. I follow it to a T in the road. The track goes left. For a moment I rebel at following this mindless heartless device. Screw it, I'm turning right. I've been watching this blue streak for days. What does it know? There may be galloping horses to the right. Maybe even a fine Barista, or a Harley rider with great oatmeal.

I pull out a map. Nope there is no town within site to the right. OK, fine, I'll follow the blue line. Rebellion can wait until tomorrow.

Earlier in the day, I had been treated to Red Rock Pass and Red Rock Pass did not disappoint. Even on this overcast windy day, its beauty stood tall, rising to heights of seven-thousand-one-hundred-feet, in the Centennial Mountains. The pass itself is fifty-six miles long of high-altitude beauty.

Roads like this were tailormade for this motorcycle. There is nothing severe to test its mediocre suspension. Gravel condition is mostly well laid and well compressed. The miles fly by, only interrupted for the occasional stop and stare moment, taking in the site in the hope of burning it deep into the brain.

The pass divides two counties of Montana, manmade lines mostly meaningless during rides like mine.

My experience traversing through this part of Montana is one of leisure, simply enjoying the scenes, riding at an unpretentious pace, content of spirit.

Worn fence lines dot the wide-open land. The grass is brown and tall and windblown. What nutrition it offers is beyond me. Still, I see a few cows.

In the distance there is a dark form, horizontal and low. As I near, its age shows.

I am drawn to old structures. These timbers were once part of a coral outpost. Long abandoned. Left to

decay as time and weather will do. I am reminded of a
John Prine song.

The people may be gone from these structures,
moved to better accommodation but the cows are still
there. The cows are, in fact everywhere in these remote
lands.

Fences and cows lead one's gaze to a wide
Wyoming sky. The horizon is as exact and rugged as the
men who built these structures, a reminder that cattle
ranching without modern equipment is an impressive
undertaking.

Marilyn has a useable fuel range of roughly 220 miles. Today's ride was 250. Luckily, she doesn't mind being my beast of burden. Though I'm sure she would prefer red shoes to red gas cans.

Northwest of Yellowstone, my GPS track took me to an intersection along the dirt and gravel. The route turned right. Except to the right, there was a "Road Closed" sign. I sat for several minutes, looked at a paper map and could see no way around the closure.

Deciding to work around as best I could, I noticed a small line on the map that led to an entrance of Yellowstone. From previous visits, I knew there was a ranger station near that entrance. Checking with the station, I learned that fires had closed most of the route I had planned on taking. So...... what the heck, take the pavement through Yellowstone, south to Jackson, Wyoming, spend the night in Jackson and attempt to rejoin the route tomorrow.

Yellowstone did not disappoint. One of motorcycle traveling unsurpassed experiences is riding a small motorcycle next to a very large Bison, meandering down the road, knowing all too well that if Mr. Bison wanted to take you out, he could do so with one toss of his massive furry head.

The day ends in Jackson, Wyoming. I was somehow not at all tired. Perhaps it's the sight of the Tetons themselves. Perhaps it's the jewel that is Yellowstone. Perhaps I was finding a rhythm. For whatever reason my spirits were high as I pull into a gas station.

I was expecting the normal fill it up, pay and maybe grab a diet coke type of experience.

I wasn't expecting to meet a Triple Crown Hiker.

Walking out of the station after paying, I notice a first-generation Kawasaki KLR650 pull up to a pump. A young man gets off and begins to fuel the bike. The luggage attached to the KLR was modest as is often the case with young men and a KLR. This was certainly the case during my own youth and my own old motorcycle.

Which proves attitude prevails over cash every time. His attire was modest. His manner was one of ease. He didn't seem rushed. Both boots and tires were full of dirt. I noticed because my own ride and myself were in the same condition.

"Nice bike." says I.

"Thanks." says he.

And that is how I came to meet Ethan.

His smile was honest. In this honesty, he expressed fears about a motorcycle breakdown leaving him stranded someplace where all that dirt is born. Yeah, I get it. A flat tire in the waning daylight hours, on the side of some mountain, with temps dropping, would seriously stress me out. I'd be forced to deal with it. But I damn well wouldn't like it. Pitch the tent and change the S.O.B. inner tube the next morning if necessary. Today, I'm also in bear country, a fact I much prefer to put on the back burner of my imagination.

Or, I could plan better and be done riding by 5pm. Old habits, like sleeping late, die hard. So, to cover the miles, I ride until an hour before dark and then aim towards a town.

As Ethan and I share road stories, he lets slip about certain hiking exploits of his. As in very long walks. Not to the mailbox and back. Unless the mailbox is two-thousand-miles distant.

He is one of a very few. A very few who have hiked the trifecta. All three big ones.

I mention that I'm riding the Continental Divide.

Ethan, "Oh yea, I walked that a couple years ago."

Me, "You did what?"

"I walked it north to south, to allow for weather."

Me, "You walked it?"

Ethan, "It was the final hike in doing all three."

Me, "All three what?"

Ethan, "You know, the three big ones."

My brain slowly nods to itself, trying to take this in. No, can't be. Who would do such a thing? I've heard of people hiking just one, but all three?

Me, "You walked Appalachian trail, the Pacific Crest Trail and the Continental Divide Trail?"

Ethan, "I did."

"Did you just tell me you are worried about your motorcycle breaking down?" I laugh.

He doesn't get it.

"If you break down, I think you can handle the walk to safety."

He catches on and chuckles.

Perspective. Even triple crown hikers lose it sometimes.

The average man's stride is 2.5 feet. Most men walk to their car, maybe across a Walmart, at most for an eighteen-hole day at the golf course. Ethan put his stride to greater purpose than most men.

I found a photo of him, online, where his expressed career goal is "professional adventurer". Seems about right.

You may be wondering how many miles Ethan has walked. Appalachian trail (2200 miles); Pacific Crest Trail, (2600 miles); Continental Divide Trail (3100 miles). Total, seven-thousand-nine-hundred-miles.

Remember, the average man's stride is 2.5 feet. So, doing the math, that's a conservative estimate of six million, five hundred forty-seven thousand, two hundred steps. One at a time. Carrying shelter. Carrying food and water. Nevermind that, some of those steps are uphill, so they don't average 2.5 feet per step, some downhill, some sideways. Likely revising the total to seven million steps. Geeze.

We say our goodbyes, wishing each other a day with no flat tires and no break downs. And no long hikes.

While completing this book, I tried to locate Ethan to ask permission to use his photograph and his story in these pages. Even with the magic of the internet I was unable. So, I do not use his last name.

Before meeting Ethan, I had been dissapointed about missing those roads which had been closed due to fire. After meeting him, I no longer cared. At least I didn't have to walk to make my detour.

A small medium priced hotel in Jackson provides a hot shower. I looked hard for a cheap hotel in Jackson, but Jackson doesn't do cheap. Jackson version of cheap is medium priced. Evidently it takes a lot of hotel dollars to stack and weave all those Elk horns in the Jackson town square.

I didn't think it had been a particularly dusty day, but the shower proved me wrong. I stood there sort of dumbfounded at the amount of dirt flowing onto the shower pan and down the drain. I must have shed a couple pounds of grime. No wonder those I met at the checkout line in the gas station kept their distance. Anyone familiar with the Peanuts comic strip by Charles Schultz would understand when I say that my look during this day was a fine imitation of Pig Pen.

Feeling fresh and alive, I walked to a small diner where guilt had me order a salad. But then again guilt only goes so far. I chased it with a cold beer. Eighteen full ounces. In a chilled glass. Pig Pen and Charlie Brown never had it so good.

There was a baseball game on the big screen television above the bar. People were enthralled. There was lots of yelling. Every now and then there were a few loud moans of disgust. I overhead one conversation between two patrons.

"We pay that SOB forty-million and he has struck out twice. "

Patron number two, "Yea, I could strike out for half that."

Insert drunken chuckles here.

Patron one, "Every year they break my heart. Every damn year."

Patron two, "If we had a brain, we would find a new team."

Patron one, "If we had a brain, we wouldn't be sitting here watching the game, contributing to the over paid bull shit. "

A pause as a new player steps into the batter's box.

Patron two, "OK, here's our guy! He's a monster with two outs, best hitter in baseball with two outs. Come on baby!"

I don't recall who won or who lost. I do recall wondering if anyone was offering forty million to ride a small motorcycle for a couple of weeks over some old gravel roads. I guess not. Maybe I'm not the best deep sand rider with two outs. Maybe I need a new agent. I'll settle for another beer.

I walk back to my hotel and turn on the television. This exercise in futility lasts maybe ten minutes. There are cheerful news anchors who can make an empathetic face on cue when reading their lines about a tragic event. there is a sitcom with lines dumber than should ever be allowed. Maybe we need a law.

Finally, I give up. History has to be more appealing.

The year was 1840.

A child was born to the Nez Perce. He began life in what became known as Oregon Territory. His father would later, some say under coercion, become "converted" to Christianity, mainly in hopes of ending the conflict between the Nez Perce and the settlers, although in fact, the Nez Perce were one of the more welcoming tribes. Only after having land treaties canceled did, they revolt. As the young man grew, he had more and more contact with those settlers who seemingly came in unending numbers into his people's lands and was for a time educated in a mission school.

As he reached manhood, he watched the interactions with the settlers reach a breaking point. In the 1870's he would succeed his father as Chief of the Tribe, being known as Chief Joseph, or Joseph the younger. His father, Joseph the elder.

In 1877, at the age of thirty-seven, he witnessed the United States breach yet another treaty which had given the Nez Perce rights to the land on which they lived.

Gold was the reason. The Army was sent to remove them. Joseph rallied his people and fled north with the Army in pursuit. They wished to join the Lakota Tribe, led by Sitting Bull to find refuge in Canada.

Chief Joseph rode north because he had "had enough".

The Nez Perce had no chance of winning. They knew this, yet still they fought. In an attempt to slow down the Army, in what is now known as the battle at Camas Creek, Joseph decided to attack the Army camp at night. He and his braves stole the Army's mules scattered the troops and killed three soldiers.

Camas Creek is two hundred-eighty-miles northwest of where I lie reading in Jackson, Wyoming.

Reading this sort of history is both troubling and inspiring. Troubling because as history often proves, a larger population wins the day, not due to right or wrong, but simply due to numbers. Inspiring because there are lessons within the deeds of Chief Joseph about when to say, "enough is enough". Win or lose, sometimes enough is enough.

Across the globe, in today's struggle for either a world economic order or countries seeking to maintain their own culture and populist identity, or to maintain personal freedoms many literal and political battles are being fought. Those opposed to government dominance are saying "enough is enough."

Back in Ridgway, Colorado, the lone rider of my dream was riding to join Chief Joseph and other tribal leaders.

The lone rider became one of many who fought with a ferocity born of no place upon which to return. He fought in the rebellion riding his strong horse, hoping to return to the woman he loved, victorious. Ultimately, after minor success and bloody battles, he and others surrendered, overwhelmed by might and by numbers. But he fought. Winning the respect of the U.S. military along the way.

Chief Joseph the elder died in 1871. His son, Chief Joseph the Younger (who was one of the leaders of the 1877 rebellion), died in 1904. He was buried in the Colville Indian Cemetery in the Colville Reservation in Washington State.

In 1926 Joseph the elder's body was moved to Lake Wallowa, Oregon, which overlooks the land he and his people once called home.

Day 6

Jackson, Wy to Pinedale, Wy

Today, I will learn that an old flame can still burn and be reminded "don't shoot the horse!"

The Day begins at the sane hour of ten a.m. Marilyn's image is now completely gone from the gas tank.

I had been warned of this. Decals and plastic gas tanks do not make for long lasting relationships. Perhaps Jordon Peterson has an idea about plastic and decals.

No worry, I brought a spare decal. It goes on easily.

It took some doing to work my way back onto the blue line of the GPS route. I wasted an hour zigging and zagging into one dead end after another before finding a road that would land me back on the route.

South of Jackson, Wyoming, the land once again becomes wilder. I've left behind the town square filled with elk antlers and bars. On the way to find the blue route, shown on the GPS, I pass Jackson Lake Lodge and stop for a moment to enjoy the stunning scene from the back patio and an overpriced cup of coffee.

Resting my blue attired self in one of the slightly reclined chairs on that patio, the Tetons are in full view not too far in the distance. Their jagged edges bring to mind an early logger's saw blade. A finer view of the Tetons does not exist. It was worth the forty-five minutes I dither away. The blue line can wait.

Back on the bike, I leave the Tetons, and once more the route turns out to be fair. No ruts or deep sand. Looking ahead is still the order of the day, there is always the chance of a deep sandy nightmare. A horrid dream I do not wish to enter. I've previously written that deep sand is best suited for highly experienced riders. I've also written that I've never met a highly experienced rider who hasn't broken multiple bones. I like my bones intact and my sand on a beach.

The day progresses nicely. The Snake River runs to my right, out of sight, but I know it is there. I veer East, leaving it to run its course. The main body of the Bridger Teton National Forest is also left behind, though I still ride its southern region.

The forest was partially named for Jim Bridger, another Mountain man called west by the money to be made in the Fur Trade. He came to the West later than Lewis and Clark and he became one of the most well-known of his breed. Bridger was one of the first to explore Yellowstone. He married a woman from the Flathead tribe and is thought to have had three children with her.

As was common in the difficult life of the times, his wife did not live into old age, instead she died from some sort of illness which manifested with fever. He then married a Shoshone woman and had another two children.

Jim Bridger lost his eyesight in his later years after he had moved back east to Missouri. He died at the age of seventy-seven, having lived as a military scout, a trapper and a guide to private groups desiring to see Yellowstone.

Hoping to make some more humble personal history, I press onward.

Off to my left, I pass Antoinette Peak, then Triangle Peak and finally Tosi Peak. I pass these and lesser peaks, into lesser valleys and around curve after curve. Each one revealing a new understanding of the Wyoming high country.

Earlier in the day, an old understanding merged with a new one. I had to look twice to believe my eyes.

Deja vu all over again.

The United States has 2.3 billion acres of land. The odds of being in the same acre twice, fifteen years apart, once on a motorcycle ride back from Alaska and the second time on this ride has to be infinitesimal. Yet here I am.

Fifteen years ago, Richard Grubenhoff and I rode motorcycles to, from, and throughout Alaska. While in that amazing state, during a spell of unusually fine weather, I used that weather window to ride a lovely red and white BMW R100GS-PD up the haul road, 450 miles of dirt and gravel from Fairbanks to Prudhoe Bay at the Arctic Ocean. Stunning scenery. And stunning mosquitos.

I made the ride in one day. Why? Because I didn't want to test the weather, which was good at the time but could change, at these latitudes, very quickly. So, I rode. And I rode. Using the weather and the excellent gravel road conditions to cover those 450 miles.

The last two hundred miles were made in dusk. The sun rested on the horizon for eons. It finally sat, but gently so, leaving behind a rocking chairs worth of light all the way to Prudhoe Bay.

My arrival in Prudhoe Bay at 2am was a fortunate one. I had not called ahead. A hotel room was thankfully available.

The next morning because the weather was still perfect, I rode the 450 miles back to Fairbanks, moving on in a haul ass kind of day, to make sure I didn't get caught out in cold or rain on the insanely desolate road that is the haul road.

Upon return to the lower 48, the BMW and I made our way through Yellowstone, through Jackson and then visited a place called Brook's Lake Lodge, for a few days of rest.

What has this to do with 2.3 billion acres of land?

Today, following the blue line, along the Continental Divide, I look up to see..... Brook's Lake Lodge.

The first time, I came here with the specific intent of doing so. This time, I arrive completely by accident.

Brooks Lake Lodge was and likely still is a dude ranch catered mostly to horseback riders and fly fisherman. A grand lodge adorned the acreage. Scenic trail rides and fine meals kept guest content.

Once I realized where I was, at the sheer incredulity of it, I took a photo and texted it to the lady with whom I had visited the lodge. We were no longer together; but I thought she might appreciate the memory. Perhaps, I didn't think it through properly before hitting the send button.

"Look what I just stumbled upon, without even realizing I was near."

Her reply, "Somebody is trying to tell you something." But she didn't mention what. So, I rode on.

I remembered the lodge as I rode.

Within the lodge, on one massive log wall in the gathering room, the stuffed heads of at least fifty horned animals gazed into perpetuity.

Successfully hunting each species, at the time, was both a masculine definition of its day and an affirmation of a certain social status. Having one's name entered into the records of the association who administered its logbooks, was a prestigious event. I make no judgement on hunting itself. I have hunted and have enjoyed its fruits on the dinner table.

Today's hunters are not bound by the same definition of manhood success, and few aspire to line their walls with every species across the globe that happen to sprout horns, thus ensuring their place in the records of a decade's old definition of manhood.

One evening, during my visit, over a well-aged scotch, another guest, whom I did not know, and I sat in the "trophy room".

Her gaze took in the scene along the walls, and I could see her distain. Finally, she said.

"They should take those damned things down. My grandfather was also a *hunter*." she said the word with extreme distain. "He also has animal heads on his wall back home in Nebraska."

I was reluctant to enter the aura of family history, knowing very well that no family is a perfect blend of love and encouragement and that taxidermy on a wall, to this lady, may well represent far more than a hunter's success.

She was silent, expectant of some sort of reply.

"Your grandfather didn't contribute to the extinction of any of those animals. They all live and thrive today."

She moved slightly in her seat, slightly rising, ready to defend her position, how dare I challenge it.

I beat her to the mark, raised my glass in her direction, "Are we really talking about all of those stuffed heads up there? Or is this about something else?"

I could see her eyes fixed upon the ice in her glass. If a stare could melt ice, hers would have boiled it. I said nothing. She said nothing. Then, her face changed. It became softer.

"I loved him. He was a hardworking man. He had a great family. But why did he have to kill all of those animals?"

Sitting in this room, among those horns on the wall, she wanted to garner respect for this side of her grandfather but was unable to fake it.

I sat there, unsure of what to say, but just as sure that she wanted more of an explanation than I had offered. It was not my job to defend this man who I had never known.

But sometimes I'm an idiot.

I added, "Maybe view that wall as a monument to his strength and determination. You and I will be judged by generations who have no idea what the cultural norms are today. We go to the grocery story. Your grandfather and his father might have gone to the forest for some of their food."

She raised her eyes from the glass. I could see an internal struggle and wondered once again if we were really talking about hunting.

She said nothing for a long time. Finally, her glass empty, she looked up at the wall once more, then back to her glass. "I know he brought home deer for the freezer. It's just so cruel. But maybe men of his day knew what they knew. Maybe we know more today."

Back from an errand, her husband joined us and we sat for an hour, as they told me that three generations of their family had vacationed in this part of the West. They spoke of the good horses they owned, good friends and of their own children.

Today, as I ride this Continental Divide, it had been a decade and a half since I'd contemplated the stuffed heads on the wall.

If I had had a glass of single malt scotch, somewhere in the luggage strapped to Marilyn, I would have raised it to good horses and to hopefully good children and to things someone is trying to tell me.

Life may be a song, but it's also a circle.

Hindsight is 20-20. Unless, like today, as I write, one eye has a cataract, then hindsight is both lop sided and fuzzy.

After those six days of riding, my body and my mind had begun to tire. Memories of past relationships had my mind occupied. Then a squirrel scurried across the gravel refocusing my attention.

A mistake here would have consequences.

High into the Rocky Mountains of Wyoming, Marilyn clambers across rocks the size of coffee mugs. Rocks that have slid down a small scree field and now are covering the path before me.

To my left the land falls away at a forty-five-degree angle, its descent terminating a hundred feet below. Marilyn's suspension is working overtime, bouncing, and compressing from one irregular rock to the next.

Atop a small hummock, I pull over. The air is pure. It's fifty-eight degrees. The view encompasses a snow-capped peak to the west, likely topping out at over fourteen-thousand-feet. To the south, gravity has rolled an endless array of cragged soccer ball sized stones, all part of an endless erosion. A few million years from now, the Rockies will likely have crumbled into and beyond that distant valley below.

Time is trying to tell them something.

The wind picks up its pace. Clouds are forming to the west. It's time to move on, towards lower altitudes and a welcoming hotel.

     I ride on. I listen to the motorcycle. Marilyn withholds her memories. I capture mine on digital film. The gravel turns, gains altitude and becomes crevassed by small washouts. I take care to avoid the ones caused by drainage flow parallel to the path. An hour passes. Then two. The road opens, vistas now wider, in contrast to the last two hours of tree lined pathway.

     Looking ahead I see a large truck parked to one side of the right of way. Just beyond is a horse and rider. Beyond further are a string of cows. The rider moves gracefully with the horse. No bouncing. A very good rider. The horse responds to leg cues. Shifts of weight, slight undertaking of reins. The whole movement fluid. Long rehearsed, practiced, understood. No need for drama, nothing rushed or forced.

With apology to Willie Nelson....... Cowgirls might be easy to love but they are definitely harder to hold. High altitude grazing. Round up time. Coasting, engine off. I politely asked to take a photo. She tipped her hat, yes. Ah, for a better lens.

Leaving rider and cows behind the road begins a slow decent towards the town of Pinedale. The hour is getting late, and the day has been satisfactory. Highly so. Watching a rider brings back my own poor attempts at horsemanship.

In my wallet there lies a business card, upon which there is a photo of a horse and a single printed line.

"Riding lessons by Samantha."

Earlier I had mentioned a certain black powder flint lock competition in northern Phoenix. Well, after finishing solidly in the middle of the pack, and walking across the gravel road to grab a diet coke at a small tent with treats, I heard horses. I walked closer. What I saw was something I had never witnessed.

Rider on horseback, hauling ass, popping balloons with what appeared to be live ammunition. Naw, can't be. That would be crazy dangerous. I eased up the fence line and asked someone what the heck was going on.

"They use blanks, silly."

"How does a blank pop a balloon?" I ask.

"Hot embers."

"Ahh." But I still didn't really understand. But it looked like fun.

I was going to be in the Phoenix area for two months or so, my camper and I, and after doing poorly at the flintlock event, figured maybe a new sport was in order. Like any modern person would do, I fired up the internet on my smart phone and found someone who teaches the sport. Someone named Samantha.

For the next month, I had made a pretty good intention of learning how to ride a horse. Four days a week. An hour each time. Like most things that some people are able to make look easy, it was far more difficult than I had imagined.

The goal was to learn to ride well enough to enter a competition for a sport known as Cowboy Mounted Shooting. Think of a rodeo. Now think of barrel racing. Imagine instead of barrels, there are balloons placed on four to six-foot-tall pieces of PVC driven down through the hole of a traffic cone. Instead of three barrels, imagine there are ten such pieces of PVC, each holding a balloon, thus ten balloons, spread through the arena in a pattern.

In the sport of Cowboy Mounting Shooting each rider takes a turn riding the pattern. So that riders and horses can't get too familiar with the pattern, there are over eighty different patterns. Riders don't know which pattern will be used on any given day.

The riders carry two single action revolvers, each holding five black powder blanks. Just black powder. No projectile. Cocking the hammer with your thumb, to ready the gun for each shot, then pulling the trigger, sends out a flume of hot embers, traveling about fifteen feet. The hot embers pop the balloon as the rider directs their horse through the pattern. The balloon will only pop if your aim is good and you are close enough to the balloon.

So, mount up. Walk your horse into the arena and gather your thoughts and your nerve. You see the timing line that once you cross will start the clock.

You know that when you complete the course and return to the timing line the clock will stop. You also know that the particular pattern you see in front of you has been completed and all balloons popped by the top riders in under fifteen seconds. This, you try not to dwell on.

Your attire is period correct as the rules require. You wear chaps to protect you from an errant black powder burn. Your hat is pulled down tight. You begin a slow circle, on the correct lead so that your horse is set up for the first turn in the pattern. The correct lead referring to which foot the horse lands furthest forward in relation to the direction of the arch you want to ride towards the first balloon. If your horse is well trained, your foot and body cues will ensure the steed is on that lead. If you mess this up, you will likely look quite ungainly as you try to get yourself and your horse back under control.

You run the entire ride in your head, seeing that first balloon, then the next and so on. Knowing all too well, that your plan is only a plan, you must adapt to mistakes, both your own and your horse's, taking a balloon later than you had intended, adjusting the arch of your ride here and there, slowing when necessary to maintain distance from each balloon so that when you shoot, you are close enough to allow the hot embers to do their job. Your desire to take each balloon sideways to your horse. Shooting over your horse's head will not make its day and the resulting reaction on your horse's part could ruin yours.

It's too late to think of the basics of riding. If they are not well ingrained by now, you will falter badly and your ride will not be a competitive one. Heels down, rein hand low, this is after all a one-handed rein event because you need your other hand to shoot those balloons. Your horse has been trained to react to just the slightest pressure of those reins on one side of his neck or the other, or a soft touch with your foot, or both.

There are 24 divisions. Levels one through six for men and women, and then a one through six for senior men and senior women. You hope to be competitive within your division, like a handicap in golf, riding against those of similar ability and on horses of similar training and speed. Riders who win three of their division events move up one division. Those in the top number six division ride at a pace that is truly frightening to the uninitiated.

What could go wrong? Your horse could stumble. Your riding skills may not be up the quick turn necessary, while looking behind you and shooting that balloon as you ride away from it, at near full gallop as is the case for the top riders. If your balance is subpar you could end up in the dirt. Maybe you don't cock the hammer in time, or fully, for an upcoming balloon and miss it entirely, making your aim late for the next balloon which you also miss.

You carry a holster around your waist. There are two leather sheaths with a revolver in each. After your first five shots, you must, while still riding the horse, place the first revolver back in the holster, preferably without looking, then remove the second gun from its holster, while you guide your steed towards the sixth balloon, which is likely not in a straight line from the fifth balloon, many of which are just around the bend of full one hundred eighty degree turn, as you sit back helping your horse squat for the turn and launch you out of the turn, their powerful hind quarters engaging in a full on linear motion, because you have trained them well. So, now you try to anticipate the launch by shifting your weight forward and off the horse's hind quarters, all the while keeping your eyes on that sixth balloon, so you can once again cock the hammer, and pull the trigger when the balloon is approximately at a ninety-degree angle to you and your horse. Not too close. Not too far away.

You are nearly there, you and the horse are now flying full bore towards the final balloons and the finish line, taking each balloon in sight, making each one count as if it's the only one that counts, because for every one you miss, you incur a five second penalty.

You press on, the horse under you gaining momentum as you ride, doing what it does so easily, with so much power that there is no way to overpower it, you can only balance it, ride it, guide it, hopefully in sync with its movement as finally you pass the timer and circle the horse before it careens headlong into the fence. Oh, yea, and that circle should only be in the direction of the last arch necessary in the pattern. It is poor form and poor horsemanship to turn the horse leftward after passing the final timer, when the last turn in the pattern was rightward. No one, except your trainer will mention it, but everyone will know. It's a polite crowd.

You holster the second revolver during that final circle, wait for your breathing and your heart rate to subside, come back down from the intensity of the ride and guide your horse out the gate where you blend with the other riders awaiting their turn in the arena.

Easy as pie. Or so I thought.

After the first ride through the course, you return to your trailer to rest. There will be two more stages to this day's competition. Two more chances to shine. The course will be changed each time. There are over eighty courses in the sport. You never know before you arrive which courses will be used.

Learning any new sport is always a challenge. Even the world's best athletes often struggle with a new sport. Some of the best at basketball can't hit a golf ball worth a damn. Others who send little white golf balls three hundred yards down the middle of the fairway can't shoot a free throw within a foot of the hoop.

I was about to learn my own limitations when it came to horses. My goal of entering a beginner competition in Cowboy Mounted Shooting was asking too much, too soon.

Instead, I was gracefully offered the chance to provide evening musical entertainment at a Cowboy Mounted Shooting event in north Phoenix. Balance on a guitar is far easier than on a quarter horse.

A couple of weeks into the lessons, I admitted to myself that even though I wanted to learn the technique of horse riding, I mostly continued those lessons for almost two months because of Samantha.

Sam is a hell of a rider, shooting balloons on her well-trained mare as if it's a common everyday occurrence. Brunette hair. Intellect as sharp as a hook and a wit sharper still. Life experiences that had required early adulthood and responsibility. The saying wise beyond their years was coined for Samantha.

Somewhere around the tenth lesson, I demonstrated my innately smooth athletic ability and fell off the horse. Bella, the mare, was going very slow. The ground was thankfully soft. It wasn't Sam's fault. I would likely have fallen off the quarter operated one at the local mall.

And that, is how a certain business card came to be in my wallet.

For all the guys out there, who have always wondered why women often make better riders than men, I offer this lesson in physics.

Men have a lot of mass above the belt. Many men have relatively short inseams compared to most women. Mass up high, on a horse ain't the recipe for good balance. Long legs and less mass up high are a huge advantage.

So, falling off really wasn't my fault. That's my story and I'm sticking to it.

Back to dirt roads. Back to gradually descending altitude. To the West lies Clause Peak then Hoback Peak, each making an impressive statement.

The day, as days will do, takes on a cadence, easy in the morning, picking up pace mid-day, then slacking off again as the sun makes its own way towards the western Wyoming sky.

For reasons unaware, today I ride with a contented feeling. The sounds, the trailing dust, the engine vibrations, even the air through my helmet all combine to hypnotize the day into serenity. Miles and miles go by without true awareness. I see, yet I do not. For parts of the day, I am aware, but only in a peripheral sense. Harmonic pulses from six hundred fifty cubic centimeters of a large air pump called an engine, fill my body and my head like warm water fills a bath tub, leaving my spirit clean.

Then, just as I look at the odometer and become aware of the miles that were once in front of me and now are behind, the road as it often does, on this route spits me out onto pavement. In a blink the world changes. Traffic whizzes by. Noise levels increase. Certainty of pace and ease of movement become more frantic, searching for signs, speed limits, watching for cars, people, racing the sunset. Everything has changed. From a spirit riding through quiet countryside to a mere man in search of a hotel and a real-life shower.

The pavement leads to one of Wyoming's most interesting towns. Pinedale. Where metal musicians play for tips on main street and the memory of mountain men linger on.

Pinedale rests at seven thousand one hundred seventy-five feet above sea level and has a population of just under fifteen hundred people, the town growing considerably in the summer as the tourist arrive.

One of the attractions is the Museum of the Mountain Man. The Museum is the final home of one of Jim Bridgers rifles. The Museum began in 1990 as a tribute to the men who came west during the fur trade years, a period which lasted only twenty years, with approximately three thousand men who journeyed the territory in search of beaver pelts and themselves.

No one would dare enter such a treacherous occupation in such wild and dangerous country without hearing an inner calling. I wonder if this voice has become a mere whisper as the century has passed from an outdoor self-reliance to a cubicle and a computer screen.

The popularity of "adventure bikes", a trend that I believe is partially due to a rebellion of men to being defined by that cubicle. The "Call of the Wild" heard by Jack London may not be the same call heard today, but it's a call nonetheless.

Motorcycle riders of the 1950s and 60s were often labeled as outlaws. I am sure there were a few bad hombres, but I suspect most simply heard the call away from the coal mine, the assembly line, the farm or the office. And a Harley Davidson was their bike of choice.

There was no such class of motorcycle as an adventure bike. Each generation seeks their own definition what is cool and what is not and their own definition of bike of choice, and if their dad rode it, they likely won't. Harley is wise to enter the dual sport market.

I feel at home in Pinedale and its Museum is like a light left burning for an expected traveler. I need not don buckskin nor is it necessary to fire round ball towards big game to make my meal.

I stop at a two-story wooden hotel, shower and change into blue jeans and a T-shirt and walk through the town. It's chilly, so I wear the blue jacket.

I am met not by a mountain man but by a rusty fellow playing guitar in front of a restaurant. How did they know that would be just the thing to get me inside.

"Three chords and your smile.". So goes the song written by Dave Potts, songwriter extraordinaire. Dave lives in Alabama, but I don't think he would mind if Mr. Tin Man were to play his song. While he is at it, I hope Mr. Tinman also plays, "One Mississippi", also written by Dave Potts.

This is a musician who could use three cords and a quart of W.D. 40.

After paying homage to Mr. Guitar Tin Man, I realize that it's still early. I could use a coffee but don't want to be awake all night.

When the waitress arrives, I order a half-caf, thinking this could be the first half step in a 12-step process. The lady actually laughed out loud.

"You must not be from around here."

"What gave that away? My jacket or the wimpy drink I just ordered?"

"Well, both actually."

"I'm trying to cut back on the caffeine."

"Why?" was her reply.
"Good question." I say.

She was not fashion model slim. She was not fashion model tall. She wore black tight stretch pants and a black flowing top. Around her neck was a gold chain, its ornament tucked into the shirt. I wondered if it was a leaf.

Me, "What sandwich do you have that goes well with a cup of half-caf?"

Her, "I could cut one in half." When she laughed at her own joke the gold chain bounced revealing its dangle. A Simple dollar sign, in gold, to match the chain.

I had seen this symbol before, immediately taking a liking to this fifty something lady. I wondered how many of her other patrons imagined its significance. Ayn Rand lives on.

Me, "Ok, you win, cut it in half then give me both halves. And let's go with a cold beer instead of the half-caf."

Her, "You might fit in here after all."

For a moment, I'm self-aware, hoping no one near overheard my half-caf order. A meal needs a newspaper. Meals still exist. Newspapers not so much.

The free Wi-Fi becomes my digital paper.

The year was 1773.

A boy who was is destined to play an integral role in exploring the west was born to "mixed parents".

He was also destined to meet a grisly end.

His mother was Shawnee. His father was French-Canadian. He was born in Ontario; Canada and he learned to read and write. He also learned Shawnee, French, English and a language which proved to be of greater importance, the sign language used by many native American people.

Many Americans know the names of Lewis and Clark, Kit Carson, John Colter, Jim Bridger and Jedidiah Smith.

Somewhere in the fine print of history is the name George Drouillard, a man who proved his worth to Lewis and Clark, referred to in Lewis' journal as 'Drewyer'. Lewis praised George's hunting skills and interpretive skills. Lewis says that on one day, Drewyer, brought down eight elk to feed the men.

Drouillard was twenty-eight years old when he joined the Corps of Discovery, the unit of the United States Army formed to support Lewis and Clark. Drouillard had already become wise in the ways of hunters and trappers. Today, along the Eastern ridges of the Continental Divide, Mount Drouillard is named in his honor. His sign language skills were highly valuable to Lewis and Clark.

After his time with Lewis and Clark, Drouillard was hired by the Missouri Fur Company, led by a Spanish gent named Manuel De Lisa. The now famous John Coulter was also part of the group. De Lisa would later be appointed as a U.S, Indian Agent. Even though he was already married to a European woman, De Lisa married the daughter of an Omaha Chief, perhaps to help in Indian relations, perhaps just because she wore pleasing jewelry and looked good in a deer skin.

De Lisa and Drouillard made a good team. Both having skills that mattered. But peace had not been made. Natives were growing very aware that they had been dealt a poor hand and some were determined to take revenge.

The negotiating and diplomatic skills of De Lisa would not stop the gruesome end of George Drouillard.

In 1810, at the age of thirty-seven, Drouillard went ahead of the party to scout. His body was later found by the De Lisa expedition. He had been beheaded and gutted; the gutting likely having occurred while George was still alive.

It is unknown if the grizzly deed was carried out by Blackfeet or Gros Ventre, the expedition had seen conflict with both.

Day 7

Pinedale, Wy to Rawlins, Wy

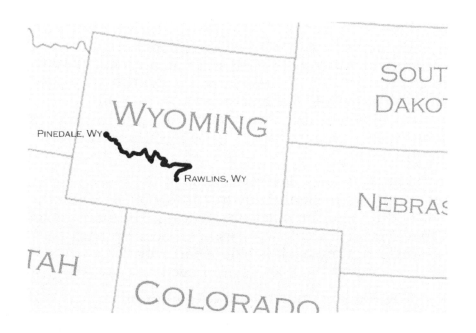

Today, I meet a liver eating mountain man.

This day begins like any day should. Yes, you guessed it, with coffee. There is a restaurant within a block of my hotel room. Thankfully, no ride necessary. I stumble there, mumbling to myself, wiping the sleep from tired eyes, feeling remnants of dust. I could have sworn I took a shower last night. Maybe it fell out of my ear.

A happy lady led me to a table, in the back, away from the other patrons. Maybe I didn't take a shower.

She didn't seem to mind. Her happiness should have been contagious, but it was early.

I ordered two eggs over well, bacon, crispy hash browns, coffee and a side of diet coke. I was in nirvana. Even their wi-fi worked well. This is perfect. I could sit here all day.

I see a sign. They close at noon. I almost cried. The bacon arrived and saved me.

Today, my own stress will be limited to the weather, which is cooperating and the mechanical well-being of the motorcycle, which, so far, is also cooperating. I would learn soon enough that my mechanical diagnosis abilities were not up to the task of a motorcycle trying its best to leave me stranded. More on that later.

I need an easy day. Even though the route has been mostly sit back and daydream sort of easy, still the miles add up and the miles are wearing. The suspension on this DR650 is stock. My legs are stock. My back is also stock. But my back is older than both the shocks and the seat and the bike itself. I need an easy day.

The rough plan is to make it to Rawlins, Wyoming, and the conditions are divine.

Before leaving town, there is something I need to attend to.

I walk from the breakfast establishment through town until I once again find the tin man guitar player. After taking his photo, I fold a dollar bill and slide it between his fingers into his guitar. It's not much of a tip, but it's the largest one he's ever had.

Back to the hotel. Once more I put on the attire of the dusty road rider. When sliding on my left boot, I notice the sole has begun to come loose from its base. Ah, the joys of stuff that is made somewhere by someone who is under the supervision of someone, all of the someone's not much caring about the quality of the product. These boots are three years old. They have six thousand miles on them. In my tool kit, I have a product called "Shoe goo", which is basically thick glue. Tonight, I'll put it to use.

The soles of these boots are not stitched to the upper portion, instead they are glued. In the last ten years or so, I can count five pair of various shoes which soles have come unglued. Ain't "made in

China great?"

In the meantime, let's ride. The route today begins on Highway 191 which is paved. It then veers East at the settlement of Boulder along Route 353 through ranch land, wide open riding, allowing for fast speeds. I ride over Silver Creek, southward crossing Haywire Road, southward still crossing Cottonwood Creek then turning east again then southeast to cross the East Fork River.

Highway 353 becomes Big Sandy Elkhorn Road. Vegetation is brown, sparse and limited. I ride parallel to Muddy Creek for a couple of miles before leaving it behind, continuing into a vast brown sea of sagebrush. A Cadillac could traverse this section of the ride. The road is gravel, but it is wide and smooth.

The GPS beeps at me, letting me know to slow down. A left-hand turn is coming up on Lander Cutoff Road another wide-open high-speed section. The compass on the GPS shows that I'm riding east and at one-point northeast. There is no "as the crow flies" route from Canada to Mexico along the Continental Divide.

I cross Little Sandy Creek, which lives up to its name. Somewhere during the day, I pass through two small settlements. South Pass City and Atlantic City. For some reason, I did not stop at either, choosing to enjoy the good time I was making.

Somewhere during the day, I take a photo. I have no idea where it was taken, but I like the image, providing a thousand questions. Who built it? Where did they travel using it? How long was it in service? How did it end up here?

My notes and memories of the day are few. Perhaps due to the nature of the route, wide, easy riding, suited for forty miles per hour in many places, even with my limited off-road skills. I was cognizant of being alone and of being careful nevertheless good speed was made. The miles were also covered in comfort. No rain. Little wind. Sun in the sky. Easy as the pie I would eat a few days from now.

I had feared a very long day. It was thankfully not to be. Rawlins entered the horizon far quicker than I had imagined.

One of the tourist attractions of Rawlins is the Wyoming Frontier Prison Museum. I kid you not. It was that or check in to a comfy hotel. I chose the hotel. Don't judge me. It was late. Nineteenth century shackles or a twenty first century shower? Easy choice.

Rawlins, Wyoming, homes eight thousand people. Named after one of Ulysses Grant's staff John Rawlins, who is thought to have defended Grant against the charges of severe insobriety. Perhaps this is true because when Grant was elected President, he appointed Rawlins as Secretary of War. Sadly, Rawlins died at the age of thirty-eight, in Washington, D.C.

Rawlins did not come from a pedigreed background. Then again neither did Marilyn. Instead, he was the son of a poor family, whose father overdrank, hence his empathy for Grant.

During Rawlins' day, one did not attend law school, perse. Rather, one apprenticed. He passed the bar in 1854 in Galena, Illinois.

James Wilson wrote his biography in 1916. Rawlins never lived in his namesake town. He only camped there in 1867.

Rawlins is also known as a place where to hematite was mined. A type of iron used to pigment paint at the time. Hematite paint is thought to have been used as the original paint on the Brooklyn Bridge in New York City.

I find a hotel and a restaurant where; a lady of college age came to take my order. I asked if she was from Rawlins.

Her, "I am, sort of, but I'm moving to California after school. My parents moved us here fifteen years ago when I was seven."

Me, "Where did you move here from?"

Her, "San Francisco."

Me, "You heading back to San Fran?"

Her, "God no, I'm going to Los Angeles, I have a friend in college whose father is in the movie business."

Me, "You look the part, you should do well."

And she did, exactly like the million others who move there hoping for the movie business. But who am I to rain on her parade, she could be the next Marilyn.

Maybe she will meet a nice guy who rides bicycles along the Continental Divide. Maybe she will see his resolve and admire it.

After dinner, I check on the bike, whereupon I smell gas. Oh, shite. I had left the fuel valve on.

When I was working, the business of choice was mortgage banking. When I was in school, the study of choice was business and law. Well, after decades of trying, I learned that what I don't know about mortgage banking could fill an encyclopedia. What I don't know about business and law could fill several. Standing there, in front of the motorcycle, it occurred to me that what I don't know about carburetors and motorcycles could fill an ocean.

I closed the fuel valve, went to bed and hoped for the best. Ha Ha would be the appropriate phrase here.

Back at the hotel I turn on the computer and read.

The year was 1847.

The Continental Divide was again running red with the blood of Indians and Mountain Men. One of whom would inspire a movie.

Imagine you live in the West. You live, at least during summer, on the eastern ridge of the Continental Divide, near what is today Red Lodge, Montana. Imagine you and your family have lived there for three hundred years. Imagine you have fought other tribes for the best land. Imagine, over time, you acquire horses, learn what to eat, how and where to hunt, to fish. You know which lakes hold fish, which rivers hold good water. One day, you and your family arrive at a lake you have fished for generations. You find men there. Men who do not look like you or talk like you.

Over the next several years, through sign language, you come to live near them because they are no threat. Decades pass. Your son and your daughter now see more of them. One day at that lake, your son rides in to see men building a cabin there. They plan to stay. Permanently. Your son communicates to them that he will still come here. Their reply is to fire a flint lock rifle over his head.

Your son retreats, gathers others, returns and drives them away. Some die.

The years pass. Others come. They too begin to build cabins at the lake. Your grandson now drives them away.

Into this world rides a mountain man named John Johnson. He rides into the territory of the Crow Tribe. The Crow had been driven west by a better armed, more aggressive tribe. Originally, the Crow made their home in what is now Ohio. The more aggressive tribe were the Cheyenne and then the Sioux.

Once west, the Crow resided in Yellowstone Valley. The Crow were one of the early adaptors of the horse breeding fairly large herds. These herds were routinely raided by Lakota, Arapaho, Cheyenne, and Blackfoot.

The Crow, their sons and their grandsons were very tired of driving off new men building cabins.

Into this history of violence and theft, rides Johnson. He builds a cabin. He marries a native. For a while thing are OK. Then they are not.

One evening the cabin is attacked. Johnson is not at home.

His wife, a Flathead Indian was at home, and she was alone. They brutally kill her, leaving her bloody body to be found when Johnson returned.

Johnson in a state of fury and agonizing madness sets upon revenge. He begins to kill Crow braves. He is rumored to have killed more than three hundred Crow braves and to have first scalped them and then to have eaten their livers. Folk lore of the time supposedly held that no brave could enter the afterlife without their liver.

The movie, Jeramiah Johnson is loosely based on the life of John Johnson.

Discovering factual events of mountain men, is an almost impossible task; but one fact (if military records are accurate) is that Johnson joined the Colorado Calvary in 1864 and served for one year.

Today, in the town hall of Red Lodge, Montana, his photo hangs, as one of the towns marshals, where he served during the 1880s. Also in Red Lodge is the cabin where he supposedly lived and where his wife met her grisly end. The cabin was moved to Red Lodge from a nearby location.

Johnson, like many mountain men of the late 1800's, was not born in the West. He took his first breaths likely in New Jersey and is thought to have been born John Garrison, but changed his name after a confrontation with an officer aboard a ship, to Johnson.

Life in the West offered little security and men worked wherever and in whatever endeavor they could find. Johnson is believed to have been a sailor, a scout and a trapper as well as a gold miner. During the time he married, he likely carried a flintlock rifle or flintlock smooth bore. If he was fortunate, as shown in the movie, he would have acquired a Hawken, though hopefully under kinder circumstance than the movie portrays.

Johnson died in 1900 at a Veterans home in California, where he was buried.

Then, an odd thing occurred.

During his life he had roamed Montana, Wyoming, Colorado and Idaho. One would think that in death, he could stop roaming. But it was not to be.

For reasons not completely revealed, in 1974, a teacher in Cody, Wyoming, who had become interested in Liver Eatin' Johnson, rallied a group of 7th grade students to conduct a crusade of sorts. They ultimately were successful in bringing the remains of Mr. Johnson to Cody. All of the students persuaded the federal government to declare them his unofficial next of kin. The Associated Press ran the story in 1974. John Johnson, once more roamed into Wyoming, and the students gave him a proper burial. It is unknown where his Flathead wife is buried.

Johnson was one of many who made a temporary home in the mountains of the West, mountains that form the high topography of the Continental Divide. He and many others once walked and rode on horseback along some of the exact same footpaths upon which today's dirt roads are overlayed.

Somewhere near one of these dirt roads likely lies the remains of his Flathead wife and more than a few Crow Indian braves, some missing their livers.

I marvel at the will of men such as Johnson. I guess ya gotta do what ya gotta do, but no thanks. My trip allows me to ride just one motorcycle. I need no pack of animals rotating which one I ride each day. There is no worry about finding water and grass along the route for the animals. The men endured. They had to.

Several years ago, I endured a pleasing truck camper trip to Red Lodge, Montana, after having passed through Yellowstone Park.

Sometimes, upon entering a new town, I knock on the door of a tavern or restaurant and offer my services as a country crooner and mediocre guitar player.

I have fond memories of Red Lodge. The owner of a pizza place who shared a patio with a steak place was kind enough to allow me to entertain there. It's a favorite musical reminiscence. Montana scenery in the background. An old fireplace providing the backdrop to an afternoon and evening of three cord songs and happy tourists.

Red Lodge, Montana, in addition to being one of the most quaint and lovely towns in all of the West, is also perfectly located at the foot of one of the most well-known motorcycle rides in America, the Beartooth Highway.

There was no Beartooth Highway when the likes of John Johnson roamed the land. Only a tough as nails climb over a mountain, through a high plain then down into what is today Yellowstone National Park.

Hostility be it from wild animals or even wilder men was as much a part of the early West as frigid winters and high-altitude summers. Johnson and others like him saw more than their share.

My own ride today will be met with no hostile men intent on driving me back east or driving me six feet under.

I will meet no large bear, armed with only a slightly reliable black powder weapon. The breakfasts I have eaten on this ride may be unhealthy, and it may eventually kill me, but I didn't have to kill it.

Day 8

Rawlins, Wy to Steamboat Springs, Co

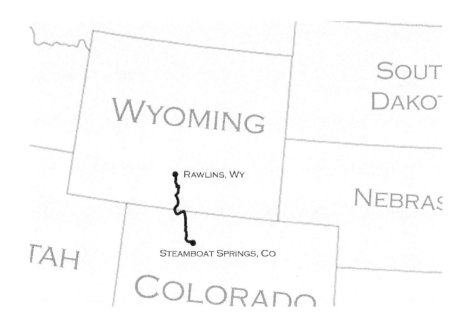

Today, I will meet a ten-foot-tall chicken and pay a visit to Adam and Eve.

After a breakfast burrito and four or five (maybe six) cups of coffee I walk outside, and politely ask the motorcycle to start.

She humors me and does so. I'm thankful but suspicious of my good fortune. I do not smell gas.

I depart Rawlins on Sage Creek Road, riding south, past the Teton Reservoir BLM campground, southward still past High Savery Reservoir, through Aspen Alley, turning West past the Sandstone Cabin.

The road is once again a thing of beauty. Miles sail by like a downwind sailing, never touching the tiller, easy as wishing upon a star. Before long, the route enters Colorado, to the South, then for reasons known only to the GPS Gods and the sense of humor that made up this route, turns northeast and quickly exits Colorado, then begins running West parallel to the border of Wyoming.

Like yesterday, a vehicle of any sort could make this section of the ride. This motorcycle is substantial overkill. I'm dusty, but comfy.

During the course of any given day, while riding a motorcycle along the back roads of America one always comes upon a sign that if not downright funny at least merits a grin.

Today's sign was both funny and pondering. What exactly would one find down a road named memory lane? The good ones? The bad ones? Sentimental ones? The ones best forgotten, those that come back at times out of nowhere, to rock you sideways. A friend used to call them "Stop light shudders", things you did, but hope you don't remember often because you shudder at the thought.

I ride on, asking the Gods of gravel roads for only pleasant memories. Further up the road at a gas station, I see what will someday be someone's orange three wheeled memory.

It seems the closer I get to Steamboat Springs; the price of memories goes up. The possibilities become more interesting. What ifs. What if I was piloting that instead of this? Could it slide around the gravel turns without landing me in the ditch? Is it comfy? Does it come with a five-foot three blonde with a trust fund and an uncle who owns a liquor store?

Street signs remind me of yesterday. The orange paint on the three wheeled contraption brings me back to today.

As I ride through today, I remember an odd place I rode through yesterday. I didn't mention it yesterday because I wasn't sure what to say. I'm still not sure what to say.

Late afternoon, on a road I do not recall, I stumbled upon a place.

Nothing much around for miles. I was making a detoured effort to find a diet coke. Just me and the antelope. And the wind. The wind that had been blowing and blowing and blowing. I saw a sign. Naw, not possible. Not out here. But in hindsight where did I think it would be?

Forty mile per hour, boreas were blowing me around like a cheap kid's toy. Maybe it was a "we're not in Kansas" anymore moment.

As I read the sign, the wind blows me to the side of the road. I park and hop off. The wind blows the bike over. I pick it up. I take the photo.

During the day, I had in my head a song, my brother Jay had put there. He had e-mailed me a song he had been working on for his own set list. The last line of which is "and I still haven't found........"

Maybe today, I found it. Here in the middle of nowhere USA. It's not the garden I had expected. Instead, it's a town. If I had been pushed, I would have admitted that I didn't think it existed. Now I know. Thing is, I had been told that it's two inhabitants had long ago been banished.

My motorcycle and I are not banished. Perhaps we should be, but we ride through anyway, straight into today's world of futuristic orange tripods posing as transport. Adam and Eve had an apple. Marilyn and I are tempted with greater comfort and faster speed.

I ride on. Steamboat Springs is just down the road. A cowboy ski town. Maybe I'll feel at home. I have a hat. I have skis. Yippie Yi Yay.

Prior to arriving in Steamboat Springs, I pass an upscale resort.

It's called Three Forks. Bill Gates would be envious. God himself would be envious. If God did envy.

My welcome committee to Steamboat is a giant chicken. Back home in Georgia (Marietta, Georgia, to be exact), there is another such large bird, perched atop a Kentucky Fried Chicken. Maybe he too moved west.

Steamboat proves to be crowded. I hear not a single yippie, nor even a yay. People stroll the sidewalks darting into shops and restaurants, filling their vacation with T-shirts and tacos.

I find a corner café, park Marilyn outside and am escorted to a comfy booth. The menu is sparse but complete. Chicken chili, a variety of sandwiches and desserts and diet coke. I order the chicken. It wasn't ten foot tall but was excellent.

What more does a guy need? The wi-fi says there is a reasonably priced hotel just down the road. I've booked a room before the chili arrives.

I can see the motorcycle parked through the window. I never tire of its lines, the way the large gas tank is suspended on the frame, the tanks large wings surrounding the big single cylinder engine, itself nine to ten inches above the pavement where purpose-built tires are planted. The entire thing screams "come on boy, let's go!" I had the same feeling two years ago when I first laid eyes on one. I still do.

Today's waitress is a waiter, in his early twenties with shaggy hair but sharp eyes. He wears the long hair with the pride of one stating his own revolt against normality. I didn't want to tell him that we wore the same hair in the seventies. What goes around comes around.

His jeans are fashionably faded, slightly torn at one knee. Atop the jeans he wears a starched and pressed white shirt, with sharp creases running down each sleave, completely at odds with the torn jeans. He wears a blue cotton buttoned up vest with neat lapels, a blue bow tie and a flat cap, also known as a Scully Cap or an Ivy cap. Picture an English driving cap and you have his headwear in mind.

None of the other waiters wore similar dress, so this was not an establishment requirement. He presented both rebellion and style, offending no customer, endearing to most. He was efficient, polite and attentive without being a suck up. This kid could go far.

He notices my jacket and my helmet in the booth seat opposite me, hesitates for a second, unsure, after all he is working, doing his best to play the role of friendly but not too friendly server. Then he sees the motorcycle out the window and can't help himself.

"I'd be down for that. What is it?"

Unsure of the lingo of today, I wasn't certain if being down for that was a good thing or a bad thing. Then his face gave it away. A good thing. So, I reply.

"It's a Suzuki DR650, built to climb mountains. One was sighted on Everest not long ago."

He picked up on the joke quickly.

"Yea, right. But it sure is nice."

"Do you ride?" asks I.

"No, but my roommate does. I've ridden his once or twice. He wants to ride to Wyoming. His looks kind of like yours."

"I just came from there." Says I, "Tell him to do it."

"Hard to get the time off work."

And that, even at his age, especially at his age, sums up the entire thing.

"Buy one and go with him." I can't help but stir the pot. Because I know. There is no way to tell him what I know, but I know.

"Maybe next year, we graduate next year and our parents want us to go to grad school, but maybe we can take some time off before. I may or may not go to law school. I've been accepted but I'm not sure."

He did not mention the name of the law school which had accepted him. I recognized the omission. No one accepted to Yale leaves out Yale in the sentence, "I've been accepted to law school."

My own law school was neither Yale, nor Harvard, nor any school, anyone, anywhere would recognize, so I understood.

"If I go, I'll have to take out student loans, but I'm not worried."

He leans closer, "isn't the government going to cancel all the loans and stick it to the banks?"

A fellow waiter, older with some grey in his hair, hearing the conversation approaches and adds this,

"Well, not exactly. The banks still get paid. You just won't pay them. Your parents and every other person paying taxes will pay the banks."

My waiter says, "that's not what I heard, I think the banks get screwed, and I'm ok with that."

The interloping waiter replies, "The banks pay politicians, you really think the politicians are going to screw the banks?"

My waiter makes a face that says, well I'll be damned. Now he gets it.

I change the subject back to motorcycles, "take that ride. Your parents will forgive you. Go during summer break."

"They would disown me. But maybe."

I know it will not happen. I've been there. The pull is too strong. The chase for the degree has a life of its own and will not be denied. Just one more degree and I'll have it conquered. Little do we know at the time that it's only the beginning. Only the entrance fee to the game.

"Where are you heading?" He is still curious. The blue jean guy leads the way, Mr. bow tie is just for show.

Me, "The border of Mexico."

Bow tie. "Dang, that's a long way."

Seems like it, but just ride for one day. Then the next. Keep doing that and you find yourself a very long way from where you started."

The older waiter, still listening, says, "Sounds like my life."

Bow tie didn't get it.

How could he. And why should he? Better to not be aware of the speed of the ride, otherwise everyone his age would be out riding motorcycles across cities, states and countries and out sailing oceans to exotic places.

Nothing would ever get done. Smart phones would have never been invented. Stockbrokers would have no customers. Life insurance salesmen would have nothing to sell. Politicians would have no one to manipulate. Eden would be just a town blowing in the wind.

"Well, I hope you enjoyed the meal."

"The chili was great, thanks."

With that he takes my cash and moves on down the line, another vacationing customer is waiting.

My hotel for the evening was almost as efficient as the waiter. It was a chain, but a good one. If it wore clothes, it would be a bow tie and flat cap kind of place.

Once settled in and comfortable, the internet becomes a history lesson once again.

The year was 1871.

The Nez Perce had suffered three broken treaties. 1855, 1863, and 1868. Each time the results were less and less land for the tribe. By 1871, their numbers had dwindled, and their people were not populated in a set geographic distribution.

The U.S. Government took this as an opportunity, sending a surveyor to assign parcels to individual tribal members. The outcome, according to the Nez Perce website is why the current reservation resembles a checkerboard, with non-tribal land interspersed among tribal land.

They did retain the right to hunt, fish and graze cattle on federal, non-tribal land. As of 2022, there are more than 3500 recognized citizens on about 770,000 acres.

Also, today they operate the Clearwater River Casino and Lodge in Lewiston, Idaho; the It'se Ye-ye Casino in Kamiah, Idaho; the Zim's Hot Springs in New Meadows, Idaho; and the Red Wolf Golf Club in Clarkston, Washington. All in all, the Nez Perce are one of the top 3 employers in Idaho.

I wonder what Chief Joseph would think of all this.

Day 9

Steamboat Springs to Kremmling, Co

Today, I enter the world of marital bliss, and dirty shorts.

I had set an alarm for 9:30. And sure enough, now its silly tone was playing loud and clear. For a moment, more sleep seemed a virtuous option. Because I had heard that virtue was its own reward and surely sleep was a reward. I hit the snooze button; five times.

I don blue jeans and a three-day old T shirt with a chest patch saying, "toys for tots". I bought it at a second-hand store in Ridgway for three bucks, so it's messaging was secondary to its price. So far, no one has noticed and asked me about my young children, which I do not have, young or otherwise.

Tomorrow, I will toss it into a hotel trash can. Years ago, I learned that doing laundry on trips like these costs more than buying another three-dollar shirt. I wonder to myself if the author Lee Child is a long-distance motorcycle rider. Did he get the idea of a character named Jack Reacher tossing his clothes instead of doing laundry by making a long motorcycle ride?

The walk to the lobby was not long distance. It was a short walk for a short stack of waffles, the pour in liquid batter, flip me over on my swivel, type of waffle. There was also a machine dispensing very sweet orange juice. I sample both. Both are OK. Both serve to raise both my blood sugar and my eye lids.

After I fully awaken, I'll deal with maps and GPS routes and all the rest. The bikes chain needs adjusting. I have the necessary tools. What I lack is the ambition. But today is the day. Guaranteed. Now, just one more waffle and two more cups of itsy-bitsy Styrofoam cups of coffee.

An obviously married couple walks in and occupies a nearby table. They began discussing the finer points of visiting the in-laws. Neither noticed nor cared if their voices were loud enough to be heard by everyone in the breakfast nook, which at the moment was only me.

"We will only be here three days." Says the wife.

"Ever spend three days in hell?" Says the husband.

"You didn't have to come." Says the wife.

"Your mother would have just come to visit us, so what's the difference? He replied.

"Why don't you just go fishing?" Was her retort, spoken with enough sarcasm to fill an outdoor stadium.

"*That* is a great idea." He rose and was gone, soon thereafter to be followed by her.

Not five minutes later, another couple came into the breakfast area. They were about the same age as couple number one, but that is where the similarity ended. They spoke softly to each other, both still sleepy but both obviously attentive to the other, not in newly dating way, but in a caring manner.

The husband poured two cups of coffee. Into one, he poured milk and emptied the contents of a sugar package. Into the other cup, he poured only milk. Then he carried them to the table while the wife browsed the bagels. He placed one cup in front of himself and the other in front of the chair for his wife. The message was clear. He knew how she took her coffee.

She sat, looked at the coffee and said, "Thank you, honey."

No one discussed fishing.

In a future life, I'd like to create that couple. Maybe they know Jordan Peterson, but I didn't ask.

I opened my computer to learn of history, long before Styrofoam. As I read, I pondered age differences, the speed of life, unobtainable models and the ability of some couples to rise above it all.

The year was 1845.

Pioneers traversed the Oregon Trail in numbers that the first Nez Perce to meet Lewis and Clark could have never imagined. Most began in Missouri and were headed for Oregon. They traveled by foot, by horseback and by wagon. The trail was first braved by fur traders and mountain men who using the tools and firearms of the day, worked their way west and back east with the fruits of their labors.

The Oregon Trail had many side trails. Historians believe that from 1840 to 1863, over four hundred thousand settlers made their way along these routes. Imagine the impact this had on the relatively small tribes of the Nez Perce.

Before the hoards came, the mountain men traded mostly in harmony with the various tribes. The Nez Perce included. When the fur trade fell off, due to over trapping and changing demand for beaver, many mountain men, like Jim Bridger and Kit Carson became Army scouts, using their knowledge of the land to further their income needs.

Many of these mountain men rode mules, a hybrid animal. Mules are sure footed in mountainous terrain and are considered better pack animals, though in open terrain, those same men preferred horses due to their faster, more comfortable gait. Horses and donkeys are different species. A mule is the offspring of a male donkey and a female horse. A female mule is often called a molly mule and a male mule is referred to as a horse mule. A gelded mule is called a John mule.

Due to an "uneven" chromosome count, mules are ninety nine percent sterile, so another mule can only be had with another male donkey and another female horse.

The Nez Perce preferred horses, and horses they rode throughout their encounters, from Lewis and Clark.

The year was 1855.

A treaty is signed. A part of which is a lame attempt to influence the Nez Perce towards the habits and customs of the settlers. In an exchange for some of their land (7.5 million acres) the government provided such thought to be desired items as a carpenter shop, a tin shop, two schools, and of course money.

There were fifty-six separate tribes in the Nez Perce world. Each leader of each tribe was bribed with five hundred dollars a year for a twenty-year period.

The United States also wanted some of the land to build a railroad.

As I read this history, I almost laugh out loud. Today, politicians still bribe those who's favor they seek. Free education, free child care, free this, free that. Paid for by others, not the politician. Never have they voted themselves a cut in pay in order to fund all the freebies.

All the while they vote themselves healthcare for life, exorbitant retirement packages, tax advantaged income for their supporters on Wall Street, insider trading stock tips and a seat at the table of high paid corporate boards for their children. Pennies for the population. Millions for those in charge.

Shame went out of style way back when in a garden named Eden. Maybe that is why the town is so sparsely populated. Few meet the standards.

Those Nez Perce who received the money are not around today. I'd like to ask if the bargain was worth losing the land.

Closing the computer, I look once again at the map. Today, I will ride from Steamboat Springs to

Kremmling. The map doesn't show what type of dirt I will endure or enjoy. It only shows lines on a paper. Each day of this ride, as I pack up and head out, I have no idea what awaits. This becomes wearing. My thoughts inclined towards worry instead of adventure. I have learned that it is this not knowing which causes much of life's stress. The Continental Divide Ride is just one more example of not knowing.

Seems to me that the early settlers had a massive dose of not knowing, which ensured that only a certain type of person made such an endeavor. Those that came later could ask those that came first: What is over that hill? What is around that bend? Which tribe should I meet with loaded gun? Which ones will welcome me? Where are the dangerous animals?

I would like to know much of the same. But I know not, so I pack up and ride, hoping for fair roads, friendly people and no man eating animals crossing the road.

Fueled with carbohydrates and caffeine, I open my tool roll and lie on my back next to the bike. Using wrench and seat of the pants measuring chain tension, the chain is tightened slightly. On each side of the swing arm this bike has lines for this purpose, making sure each side of the swing arm, where the axel passes, matches the other side, ensuring alignment between front drive sprocket and rear driven sprocket. Satisfied, I tighten the nut and reinsert the cotter pin.

Rising to one knee, more difficult than it was ten years ago, I lever myself upright and put the tool roll away, slip on helmet and textile jacket and climb aboard the thirty-four-inch-high seat. The suspension compresses and my feet are able to touch the ground.

I turn the key and hit the button. Yes! It fires to life. I am somehow always surprised. Soon enough this will not happen, not the surprise but the firing to life. But today, I am ignorant of the future.

Pulling out of the hotel parking lot, using the earth moving forty horsepower to propel us forward at a blazing zero to thirty in seven or eight seconds, I feel the day coming to life and I smile. The bike is not a highly engineered KTM, it should not induce smiles. But it does.

Route 14 takes me south through flat farmland until riding east on Route 22 for a short distance to once again turn south on Highway 40, which at one point, turns almost due north, just to drive me crazy and question if I'm on the right route. Maybe I should disable the compass feature on the GPS. Ignorance is bliss.

Highway 40 looks as if it's going to climb Baker Mountain, but instead the route becomes southerly once more on Route 19, a winding gem of a road, tree lined in places, crossing such local landmarks as Sarvis Creek and Red Dirt Creek. All of my worry was misplaced. This is as easy of a ride as I have and ever will experience. My only concern is speed. Too much thereof.

Near the point where Red Dirt Creek runs parallel to the route, I enter a left and sweeper with too much. Speed that is. Shi............ Easy boy, straighten it up, nail the brakes, bleed off that speed, then make the curve. A very close call.

After I clean out my shorts, like every rider has at some point in their riding life, I have a good talk to myself. The dialogue went like this:

"What the hell is the rush? You want to get up from one knee even slower than you do now? Slow down dumb ass."

"Screw you. I'll ride like I want. We didn't crash."

"You will never make the Mexican border, fool."

"Fine, you win."

I slow down. A few hours later of slow riding, I find myself within a few miles of Kremmling.

The Kremmling, Colorado, town website says they are proud of their rustic appeal and western heritage. They tout only an hour's drive to ski towns, thus hoping to be both remote and hip. A difficult needle to thread.

Other websites mention a population of about one thousand four hundred and a hoped for, but never found, silver mining history. Winters at seven thousand three hundred feet are long and harsh.

Because I'm now riding slower and am noticing my surroundings, I see the bright yellow mules ear flowers that dot the roadside. Further on, the state flower, columbines, make an appearance.

The area gets so much snow that young trees are buried, stunting growth. Winter temps reach forty below zero. Not the friendliest growing conditions. The trees that have adapted include Engelman Spruce, Colorado Blue Spruce and Lodgepole Pine, all similar to the high altitudes of Wyoming to the north. Quaking Aspen also endures, its white bark and gold yellow fall color making it one of the most photographed.

As I enter Kremmling I see the town is guarded by a coffee drinking cowboy. Now this is a cowboy I'd like to meet.

I ride further and see a steel woman of substantial bust. In some college towns, I imagine this statue would last about 3 days, it being repressive of flatter chested coeds and obviously created by a someone of uncertain character and Colonialism inclinations.

Dinner is a subway, eaten on the bed while watching a baseball game. It must have been an important game. The stadium was full. After the third inning, the announcers began repeating themselves, so I resorted to what used to be called the world wide web, when it was necessary to type www before every website address.

I used to know a guy named Web. For years people called him Worldwide.

I fire up google, no www required, and read.

The year was 1620.

In southwest Colorado, two hundred miles from this hotel.

Spanish explorers needed something to trade. Gold was not as easily obtainable as they had hoped.

They quickly learned of the tanned deer hides of the Utes. They also found a more profitable trade. That of humans. Women and children, the Utes had captured from the Apache, Paiute, Comanche, and Navajo.

For a hundred years this trade continued, during which time, due to acquiring horses the Utes became more mobile. Their territory expanded into Utah and Eastern California. The French explorers also began trading with the tribe.

Later, they participated in trade with the American mountain men, attending rendezvous where for several days' furs were exchanged for cloth, horses, guns and more.

I recall the exchanges of Lewis and Clark for a rendezvous with native women and consider that by the time of Lewis and Clark, such trade had been going on since at least 1620. There is no way to know what happened to the women and children traded by the Utes and by others during this period.

In the end the Utes, like all the other tribes were relegated to land which comprised of less than 7 percent of the region they once roamed.

Before being driven to reservations, they had an annual migration, over a hundred and fifty years, along with other western tribes, which created trade routes from Colorado through Utah and into California, many of these same routes in use today.

Much of the Continental Divide Ride, indeed runs along such trade routes.

Day 10

Kremmling Co. To Salida, Co.

Today, I will meet a reggae cow, named "Marley", and a man named Joseph.

But first, I have a slight panic. The hotel room has no coffee maker. The lobby has no coffee maker. I learn the difficulty of dressing without the aid of caffeine, something I hope to never repeat.

Carefully I hop aboard the bike, testing balance, finding it poor, eyes ahead, I ride.

I see a sign "Breakfast Served". I may have drooled. I pull into the parking lot and did not even remove my helmet or gloves. I nearly knock over an old lady entering the diner.

"Excuse me ma'am. They have coffee here."

"Slow down young man, they have a lot of it, they aren't going to run out."

"Sorry." And I hold open the door. Well, dang she just called me young man. Then I realized that I had my helmet and sunglasses covering my wrinkles and my hair.

Still, I take it as a sign for a good day.

A sign says, "Seat Yourself". So, I do. I find a comfy corner booth, facing the front door.

Is it just me or do all men hate to sit with our backs to a door? Look what happened to Wild Bill Hickok.

A waitress appears holding a coffee pot and a mug.

Me, "Ah coffee. I'd kiss you but I don't know you that well."

Her, "You would need to shave first, but then we can talk."

Me, "You have to excuse me, I'm an addict."

Her, "We get a lot of those in here." She gives me a menu and says, "I'll be right back."

The French toast was better than my three-day-old-bearded-self deserved. Harriette, the waitress, was nicer than my three-day-old-bearded-self deserved.

As I paid the check, she called out, "Hey, come back sometime, after you shave."

There is dirt and then there is dirt. The dirt road from Kremmling to Silverthorne, Colorado, on the way to

Salida, could be driven by your grandma. In her 1975 Buick. Cruising at 50mph. Go get em, granny. But stay outta my way. I've got miles to cover.

On to Breckenridge where a Beer Fest was in full swing and where rail was once king. Up an over Boreas Pass.

Cows. They are the reason. Without them, there would be no ranch roads. No McDouble with cheese.

I stumbled on a few cow members of the rare Reggae breed. Even their moo struck a different timing, with the accent on the 2nd beat.

I believe them to be Highland Cows, or a sub breed called Kyloe. Quick research tells me they are bred for milk, meat and just for show. The meat supposedly has less cholesterol. Their shaggy coat giving the appearance of a cow wearing Bob Marley locks.

These cows are thought to have originated in the Scottish Highlands, the breed is suited to difficult terrain and wet climates. An average male reaches a well fed one-thousand-four-hundred pounds, similar to the more well-known American breeds.

Highland Cows have a double coat, kind of like a Labrador retriever you might have at home. Like most animal herds they have a social hierarchy, older stronger males dominating, the younger always vying for position to take their place.

The Continental Divide route from Kremmling runs dead east. The Mexican border is dead south. I am suspicious but I carry on. We parallel the Colorado River for the first few miles, then leave it to our north using route 33 to make splendid time.

This is almost too easy. I feel like singing "No Woman, No Cry."

The road turns south passing Williams Fork Reservoir then east again, and once more southward. A braver rider could do sixty miles an hour here. I am not a brave rider.

Marilyn and I join Route 3 and briefly ride northeast then southeast, past Williams Fork Creek, Horseshoe Campground and the Henderson Mill.

We come to Ute Pass Road, a paved section, and I open the throttle and my visor, ducking down to accelerate, hitting an illegal speed before rising, and feeling my body press the air like a wind break, slowing the bike.

Ute Pass Road dead ends, and we turn south. Running for a moment along the Blue River. Off to my right the map shows a place of interest called "Consider It Done".

Well, not yet.

There is New Mexico, then hopefully the border. I pass through Silverthorne like a man possessed, not stopping, no waiver, ride on, ride on.

Then for a short time I'm on Interstate 70, exit interstate at Frisco, then Highway 9 to Breckenridge.

Boreas Pass reaches eleven thousand feet. At one end are the preserved ruins of Como and at the other Breckenridge. The route was built to reach gold mines, long ago abandoned. A railroad ran between the two towns from 1872 to 1938 and was converted to a road suitable for most cars in 1952.

An old steam locomotive can be found in Breckenridge, a perfect photo op along the ride.

There was a festival in Breckenridge. The town was packed. A musician friend who is a busker extraordinaire was playing in town, but I was unable to find him. The crowds and the lack of parking, even for a motorcycle, were simply too difficult.

I was able to find a quiet place for a late lunch. Breckenridge is a ski town in the winter and a mellow weather town in the summer. Seems to be equally crowded both seasons.

After lunch I check the bike for the smell of gas and, finding none, assume I'm okay. You know what they say about assumptions.

The route from Breckenridge southward is a gem. Mount Lincoln and Mount Buckskin rise to the southwest. Hoosier Ridge is closer, as is Little Baldy Mountain, both doing their best to show off. And they both succeed.

The route crisses and crosses as mountain routes everywhere do, using the contours to rise then to fall.

Today, after eighty miles of "keep moving", I turn a gravel laden corner to find a man in a yellow rain jacket, standing astride a pedal mountain bike, binoculars in hand, scanning the hillside.

His name is Joseph.

I met Joseph after a full morning of hauling ass. During which my mind would wander.

I read recently that some Nero-scientists believe our inner voice speaks to us at between 300 and 1000 words per minute. You know that voice. The little one constantly in our head.

Over the last two days, my inner voice has been saying, "keep moving".

Joseph has a different inner voice. His says, "look".

I stopped to say hello. We talked of weather, passing rain, miles to make, what we had seen. I asked how many miles he made in a day.

He told me the first two weeks he rode hard. His inner voice saying, "get this done, cover the miles".

Then, over a campfire, one night, he remembered his son asking him to write down the best piece of each day, so that one day, he could share those memories with his grandson. Joseph's inner voice changed immediately.

Joseph was fifty-one years old. This trip was a sabbatical. Something he had promised himself that he would accomplish someday. He had been thinking of this ride for thirty years.

That someday became a "go now" moment when he had a routine checkup and found what turned out to be a melanoma.

Thankfully, it was easily and completely cut out. The scar was small but the mark it had left was not.

The next day he walked into his boss's office and said, "I'm talking five months off, starting next week."

To his surprise, his boss of twenty years looked at him and, after knowing him for those two decades, said, "You must have a good reason. I'll see you when you get back." And that was it.

I had to ask, "You going back?"

Joseph, "I don't know yet."

I imagine all those scenes through his binoculars would add up and eventually give him the answer.

Me, "Thanks for the conversation."

Joseph, "Want to trade rides for a week?"

Me, "If I said yes would you, do it?"

Joseph, "Probably not."

I leave him to his binoculars. Before long, I descend, running along Tarryall Creek before entering Como, a metropolis of four-hundred people. Supposedly named when miners from Como, Italy, worked the coal mines in the late 1800s.

I pass through Hartsel and then on to Salida.

The route was as kind as the weather. Those passing showers eluded me.

Salida, like most of Colorado's towns, is more than a mile above sea level, at 7083 feet of altitude.

According to Wikipedia, Salida means "Exit" in Spanish, due to its location at the exit of the Arkansas River, flowing from the valley.

Wikipedia also says there are a fair number of poets in the town.

I didn't meet any poets, but my waitress at dinner could have won an award for the best Shakespeare sonnet impersonation.

"My mistress' eyes are nothing like the sun,

Coral is far more red than her lips,

If snow be white, why then her breast are dun,

If hairs be wires, black wires grow on her head,

I grant never saw a goddess go;

Yet by heavens I think my love as rare as any she belied with false compare."

-William Shakespeare

I ordered spaghetti and a Colorado wine, a glass from Creekside Cellars, a cabernet franc.

Our conversation was brief and business like. Her workload was full. I remembered the statue in Kremmling and wondered if my waitress was the inspiration.

The meal over, I made the short walk back to my hotel, a simple place with simple Wi-Fi. But it worked. It worked just well enough to allow for some reading. I am about to enter northern New Mexico, so I read a bit of its history.

The year was 1680.

The Spanish explorers in what is today northern New Mexico had overplayed their hand. Hanging three Pueblos accused of sorcery, a lame accusation which the catholic Spaniards used to try to control the native population, who they hoped to convert. Convert, then control.

As the methods of the Spanish grew more and more harsh, the resulting unrest was predictable.

A man from the Pueblo tribe, Ohkay Owingeh, nicknamed (oddly enough) "Pope", led an uprising. On August 21, the Spanish were expelled, many of whom were killed. The Pueblo had had enough.

Today, a statue of Popay, "Pope", resides in Washington, D.C., a poor attempt, but an attempt none the less, to remember Popay and his resolve.

The United States Government did not participate in the atrocities committed by the Spanish but give a politician a chance to signal their virtue, paid for with someone's money, other than their own, and they will vote yes, every time.

Day 11

Salida, Co. To Pagosa Springs, Co

Today, I soak in hot springs, meet a lovely lawyer, and learn that you can indeed go home again.

I awake to the sound of rain. Hard Rain. Peeking out the hotel room window, I see the full-on downpour. I pull out my route map and decide to cheat. I have no interest in riding dirt roads in pouring rain. I check the weather. The system should pass through by 3pm. I make a plan. I should feel guilty. I do not.

The map on my phone gives me several options. Then I see it. Pagosa Springs. That should do nicely. A mere 140 miles away. By the time I ease into breakfast and start the ride at the crack of noon, I should arrive in Pagosa Springs in time for a sunset soak in warm waters. What a plan!

The breakfast area of this hotel is a tad sparce, but I'm not working or riding anywhere in this rain just yet, so Styrofoam coffee cups and cellophane wrapped muffins it is.

Somewhere around checkout time, I suit up in Gore-Tex and hop aboard the bike. The dual sport tires aren't well suited for pavement in the rain so the going will be slow. My body isn't made to endure the tiny leaks that inevitably creep through zippers and along jacket collars, so I hold myself in a manner to allow the drips to do the least damage to my comfort.

I stop in Saguache and again in Del Norte to use the blow dryer in a restroom to semi dry out my "waterproof" gloves and the front of my blueberry jacket.

Highway 160 from South Fork to Pagosa Springs is a stunningly beautiful ride.

In sunshine.

Today was cloudy. None of the scenery made an appearance. In the words of the wise old Indian in *The Outlaw Josey Wales,* "I shall endeavor to persevere."

As I gain altitude on Highway 160, the road ascends into a cloud. My speed becomes maybe twenty miles an hour. My visor fogs. My glasses fog. I wipe the visor with a glove. This does little to help. Thankfully, I had worn and plugged in an electric vest. I turn it on.

The going is slow. The temperature drops. I reconsider this plan, thinking of turning around. The cloud thickens. I utter a few words that I shouldn't type. I scrunch my arms to my sides. This is warmer than leaving them hanging out in a normal riding posture. For forty-five minutes, I endeavor to persevere.

I enter a tunnel and hope the road is not frozen. The electric vest is saving my bacon. Then, I see the ski slope up ahead and I know I'm at the top. OK, maybe as I descend, things will get better.

And they do. Slowly, but they do. Sure enough, my jacket and the seat of my pants are leaking. Gore-Tex may not be made for cloud riding.

The temperature slowly rises. My attitude slowly rises with it. This was a poor decision, not one I would repeat. I'm drenched. A breakdown near the highest point of the road would have been an exercise in flagging down a car and begging for mercy. I should have stayed in the hotel.

Then again, I would not have met her.

Soon enough, I reach Pagosa Springs, and the skies clear.

I park Marilyn at the Springs Resort and making a pitstop in the men's restroom where I point the hand dryer at my head and exhale. Whew, that was not the day I had in mind.

I put on a clean shirt and comb my rather unruly hair. I approached the front desk.

A buttoned up, well-trained middle-aged gent checked me into a small room and presented a map of the grounds, explaining which hot pools were kid-friendly, which were adult only and which were open after dark.

There is a gem of a café within walking distance. Warm tea was drunk. I sat as close to the heat vent as I could.

At 6pm the sun is low.

I sit alone, up to my armpits in warm water. My eyes are closed, my head tilted back against the edge of the warm pool. This has been a grand ride. My luck has held. The bike is still working. Today has been forgotten. I drift into thoughts of another long ride, to where I do not know, but I am growing to like this sort of travel. The pool I am in is recessed unto itself. It is quiet. The light is dim. Somebody pinch me.

I hear a voice.

"Mind if I join this pool? The others are sort of crowded." The voice is soft. I had not heard anyone entering the recess.

I didn't open my eyes, but I wanted to, "Sure"

And that is how I came to know Veronica. And yes, the name has been changed.

She was on vacation from a high-priced New York City law firm, overworked and over stressed, like lawyers everywhere, my opinion, not theirs. She was also highly entertaining.

We spoke of rules of evidence, of law professors, of what we wished we had known then. We spoke of the children neither of us had, the difficulty of relationships. The ease of vacation. And even of Jordan Peterson.

Veronica was in her early forties. She had black hair; dark eyes; just enough wrinkles to show life is not always hot springs and Colorado summer weather; and a style that ensured a long list of clients. She knew more about construction contract law that one person should be allowed. Her law school was well known.

Her swimsuit was one piece and fit her well.

Me, "If I were to judge a woman by her looks, and if I were to do so with a guess based on the ladies I have met on this ride, then you belong in Montana."

Her, "Just how many women have you met on this ride of yours?"

"Only a few waitresses, only briefly, and never in warm water."

Her, "Keep talking and you might get in hot water."

I make the zipping motion across my lips.

She reminded me exactly of an old high school sweetheart. For a moment I was back there, seventeen years old, consumed. I heard Veronica speak but also heard a voice from my hometown high school. Then, I recovered and told myself to do better this time. To listen. To give a damn about something other than my own wishes. Thankfully, this comes easier with age and with the all too real understanding of those we may have hurt.

We decide to leave hot water for a warm meal. Over which she shared her past. Raised in Colorado (so I was close) educated in Texas and followed a relationship to New York City, which at first, she hated and then grew to enjoy.

We laughed at riding through Eden, wondered about original sin and politics.

Her, "I don't believe a single politician believes in sin, original or otherwise."

With that thought hanging in the air, we say our goodbyes at the restaurant. I thank her for the company and the conversation and find my way back to the hotel.

I'm too tired to read history. Tomorrow I'd like to make some of my own along this long blue line.

Day 12

Pagosa Springs, Co to Chama, Nm

Today I will meet an old Steam Locomotive and a fine old film camera. The two have absolutely nothing in common.

In order to rejoin the Continental Divide route, I had to backtrack on pavement to South Fork, and then to Del Norte, a detour of almost a hundred miles.

After which the route would take me on a very long ride up down and around two very large mountains, on rain-soaked dirt roads.

I looked at the clock it was already 10:45. Well damn. That section will have to wait until another life.

I take the easy way out and ride Highway 84 to Chama, New Mexico. I decided to ride this pavement slowly, in search of photo ops.

Why?

Because of Joseph. He had a message. The message was "You ain't likely to make this ride but once in your life. Enjoy it."

One can rationalize anything. Today, I reasoned to ride a mere sixty miles, into Chama, New Mexico. Scattered showers. A steam engine narrow gauge railroad. Reasons enough.

The sixty miles took me three and a half hours. Highway 84, then Highway 64. I stopped a dozen times to enjoy the day and the scenery. The cell phone camera was put to use. Cliff bars were eaten. Cold tea was drunk.

Somewhere along the way, I entered New Mexico. This state would be my last State on this ride and it hit me hard.

A camper awaited back in Montrose. All I had to do was point the bike north after New Mexico and ride to Montrose. Then what? A nice question to ask, but a question, nonetheless. Some have careers they need to feed. I do not. Nor do I want another one. Being a part time musician suited me just fine.

Questions lingered as the road up ahead curved, allowing for as much fun as semi-knobbies on pavement would allow. Putting answers on the back burner, Marilyn and I move south.

My hands today are warm. The jacket and pants are dry. The sun is shining. The electric vest in in the luggage. My helmet is thankfully also dry, due to fifteen minutes under the hand dryer this morning, right after the gloves were given the same treatment.

All too soon, Chama comes into view.

I had read of this town this morning over breakfast. Its greatest attraction is The Cumbres & Toltec Scenic Railroad.

America's highest elevation and longest in miles narrow gauge railroad. A sixty-four-mile ride with a choice of passenger cars, traveling between Chama, New Mexico, to Antonito, Colorado.

Cars include: the Parlor Car, a Victorian themed elegant ride; the Deluxe Car, with café seating, serving coffee and snacks; the Coach Car, a budget experience with bench seats; and, finally, the Gondola Car, with open views.

The tracks of a narrow-gauge Railroad are closer together than standard tracks, helping to lower costs. However, many consider the narrow gauge to have been a fad, based on data not proven to indeed save costs. Most narrow-gauge railroads were secondary branches to standard width tracks.

Adam Burns, in 2022 wrote that narrow gauge railroads were influenced by a gentleman named Robert Fairlie, and it survived only a few decades. Used in mining operations for tight clearances Fairlie settled on a width of three feet.

Standard width tracks of four-feet-three-inches allowed for carrying more freight loads thus ending the narrow gauge to the history books.

I see white smoke in the distance and follow it until I see a parking lot where I dismount and walk towards the smoke.

The train approaches.

About twenty photographers stand poised to capture the perfect shot. Their cameras are a mix of old and new. I recognize one in particular, a late seventies Hasselblad, a gem of its day. I recognize it because my brother is a professional photographer. His first well-built camera was a Hasselblad.

The cameras owner is still shooting film. He is the only person using a tripod. He wears a vest with more pockets than a Las Vegas magician. I study his position, hoping to learn his intent, his angle of image, the lighting he hopes to capture.

Before I deduce any of this the train approached. He steadies the Hasselblad. I steady my seventy-dollar cellphone.

The train emits a cloud of white flume from the steam engine. The Hasselblad clicks. My cellphone clicks. Three generations of technology meet.

A steam engine, a film camera, and the digital world.

Across the main street from the train station, I find a hotel. A mile away I find food, then back to the hotel for a moment in history.

The year was 1917.

Ninety-Three miles south of this Chama hotel, Mr. Ashely Pond Jr, a businessman of considerable success founded a private boy's school for the sons of wealthy parents. He located the school on a mesa near San Ildefonso Pueblo, New Mexico. He wanted to change the world one boy at a time.

He did not realize his school would change the entire world.

The area was remote. The mesa offered limited access. Most of the surrounding land was government owned. A perfect location for a boy's school, where in addition to a rigorous academic curriculum, outdoor activity, including horseback riding was stressed.

.e school was one of several "ranch schools" of
.e, seeking to educate children living in remote
, of the west too far away from traditional schools.
.c Ranch School movement was a boarding school
environment.

Mr. Pond modeled his school after The Boy Scouts of America, stressing outdoor activities, hard work and independent thought.

The Tucson area of Arizona led the way with the most ranch schools. Students came from surrounding counties and cities alike.

Mr. Ponds ranch school in San Ildefonso Pueblo gained some prominence. An architect was hired, buildings were built. One of which, a grand lodge, was constructed using a combination of seven hundred ponderosa pine and aspen, hand chosen by the Architect, Mr. John Gaw Meem.

Ponderosa pine, native to the mountains of New Mexico and indeed to other mountains in the West, is a very large species, well suited for such a lodge.

Ranch schools, as the west became more populated and as education goals changed, for better or for worse, faded into the dry air of history. But not until Mr. Pond graduated a few well-known names. Gore Vidal, William S. Burroughs, Edward Hall, Arthur Wood, John Crosby, Stirling Colgate and Bill Veeck.

Veeck owned the Chicago White Sox.

Colgate became a physicist.

Crosby founded the Santa Fe Opera.

Wood would rise to president of Sears Roebuck.

Hall became an anthropologist.

Burroughs became a well-known writer.

Vidal also a well-known writer.

Twenty-four years roll pleasantly by.

Right up until the pleasantness is replaced by war.

Hitler invades Poland. Japan bombs Pearl Harbor.

Mr. Ponds school receives a visitor. A man named Leslie Groves. General Leslie Groves.

Groves recognized the schools perfectly isolated location; the limited access due to the site being on the mesa. He recognized the usefulness of the buildings; the availability of water and he made a decision.

First, he hired J. Robert Oppenheimer.

Next, the United States government, through an action known as eminent domain, purchased the school. The Manhattan project takes the place of horseback riding.

The lodge of seven hundred trees would now be used as a dining area. The boys' quarters would now house scientists.

The nuclear race has begun.

Day 13 and 14

Chama, Nm to Abiquiu, NM

Today, Marilyn gets drunk, and I get a lesson in high altitude weather.

I awake in a two-story hotel across from the train station. On the way to breakfast, I see a microwave in the hotel lobby and wonder if it is a byproduct the Manhattan project. Probably not.

Breakfast is served a quarter mile down the street. I order two eggs, sausage, coffee and because I am feeling energetic, a blue berry muffin. I'll loosen the belt a notch. Or two.

Back at the hotel, the wi-fi is down, so I sit in the upstairs lobby and read a magazine, postponing the day. It's only nine thirty, early for me. Had I known the day's events, I would have found another magazine and gone back to bed.

The early part of the day was ideal, forest riding, gentle sweepers. The fool in the helmet thinks to himself, "this is going to be fun."

Ponderosa pine are everywhere. The motorcycle ate it up like the muffin I had for breakfast. I imagined a day of ease.

Then things changed. A lot.

The route had been gaining elevation, resulting in open vistas. The trail less obvious, seemed to split then rejoin itself further on. Several times I had to backtrack to stay on the blue line of the GPS.

Eroded potholes were everywhere forcing a slower pace. Cragged, sharp rocks grew from the soil like they had been planted in a purposeful attempt to knock me sideways and slice a tire. I slow even more, coming to a stop.

I hear barking. More barking. Cattle dogs? A hiker's dog?

I whistle. The barking stops. I whistle again. The barking began again. After five minutes the wind picked up. The temperature fell. I look upwards. The sky to the north became dark. The wind was blowing south. Well, shite. This storm was going to catch me. I didn't see it coming earlier, although what would I have done?

Then, I see lightening. I sit high on a hillside, very exposed.

Time to move.

Marilyn fires to life. With a glance over my shoulder, I pick a route through the potholes the rocks and the dry grass on the side of the path.

Boom!

A bolt hit a tree not fifty yards away. It was not yet raining. I almost crash from the shear shock of the strike. The sound was beyond loud. There was no time between the strike and the boom. The word deafening comes to mind.

Wind blew in swirls. Temperature dropped rapidly. Sky blackened. The scene has changed from benign to severe within thirty seconds.

Ride boy! Ride! Get down off this mountain. Marilyn sprang forward, willing, eager and full of grit. The tires dig and hold me on line. Dig in again, hold again. This was repeated over and over for maybe 15 minutes. I bounce and weave.

Then again. *Boom!*

This time a bit further away, maybe seventy-five yards. The sound was just as deafening. Just as full of fury and fear. The sky overtook me. Rain began to fall. The temperature dropped even more.

Ride! Keep moving. Get off the damn mountain before it kills you. I stand on the pegs. Rain strikes my face shield. Then the glasses fogged. Another not so silent curse inside my helmet. I open the visor more, allowing air flow, but also allowing droplets of rain to run down my chin and neck, inside my jacket.

The sky lightened, turned oddly white. The clouds were higher. The rain stopped. For a moment, I breathe a sigh of relief.

Then it hails. Hail the size of my thumbnail. Gentle at first, almost fun. Then the temperature fell another five degrees and the sky became a little demon child throwing white pebbles in a temper tantrum.

During all of this I had somehow made my way to a slightly lower altitude, with thousands of trees to the left and right of the path.

I pull over, see a particularly dense section of trees, lean the bike against the nearest one and sit my butt under the branches, providing an immense umbrella. An umbrella that I hoped didn't attract lightning.

I sit and watch as the path I'd been riding turns into a solid white mass of fallen hail.

Then, it was over. Gone. Just as fast as it had come. It left a slippery mess in its wake.

I shiver and realize the lightening and the rain has rattled my cage and soaked the front of my shirt under my jacket. I shiver again. I could hear the conversation.

"Well, Ma Fletcher how did your son meet his end?"

"Near as we can tell the lightening missed the boy, but he succumbed to hypothermia. Damn shame. He was only thirty miles from a hotel and had plenty of gas."

I dig out a fleece jacket, remove my wet shirt and shiver once more. I read somewhere that in times like these you should hug a naked person for warmth. I scan the horizon. No one appears. My luck it would be an old rancher on horseback.

"Son, you can hug the horse, but you ain't hugging me."

So, I did a few jumping jacks and thought of warm resort hot springs and lovely lawyers.

Body heat, thanks to fleece, returned. I pluck Marilyn from her tree and ride on. The sky turns blue. The temperature rises. What the hell just happened? In the span of twenty minutes, I'm dodging lightening, hypothermia and now the day looks like something ordered up for a movie shoot.

I turn the corner, thinking I now have it made. Well, maybe not. I look ahead and see a mess. A tall, rocky mess. A hundred yard climb full of softball sized rocks lies directly in front of me.

This section of the Continental Divide Ride has since been changed and rerouted. Evidently, the hundred-yard uphill crawl and bounce over softball sized rocks was drawing complaints. I would have complained but didn't realize anyone would listen.

The good rider on expensive suspension would have little issue in this section. My tired, antiquated DR650 was up to the challenge but just barely. More likely, I wasn't up to the skill set necessary to make it a walk in the park. And I was still cold.

I rest at the bottom for a good ten minutes, warming up my body and my nerve. Then, I glance up the hill.

Three guys on dual sports were at the top, riding north, looking down. They too pausing, wondering just what they had gotten into. One by one they rode down, making it look easy. Each pulled alongside my bike. They had not seen the hailstorm. It missed them entirely. Go figure.

One of them said they were headed to Moab. I asked if they were going to stop at 3 Step Hideaway and they said, "Well, Hell Yes!" It's a small world.

I gave the them my music performance card saying, "Give this to Scott and Julie. Tell them you found it nailed to a tree halfway up this damn hill."

"Second thought, leave out the damn, Scott and Julie probably wouldn't appreciate the language." I sold myself.

The bike and I made it up the hill. Pick a line, give it some throttle and hang on.

After the lightening, after the hail, after the uphill rocky nightmare, the route widens, some of it is paved. Life is back to easy. No more rocky hills.

While still on pavement, the route passes through El Rito, New Mexico, where I see a sign. The gentleman must have had his own time on a high exposed mountain. It greatly affected his attitude.

By the time I reach Abiquiu, NM, I have ridden only one hundred ten miles. It took me eight hours. A whopping 13 miles per hour on average. A challenging day. But oddly rewarding. By far the toughest day on the trip. Marilyn is, now, somewhat untidy.

At long last, I reach my hotel for the evening. The Abiquiu Inn, home of the Georgia O'Keeffe Museum. A welcome site.

There is nothing much around the Inn. A gas station one mile away. The former home of the famed artist Georgia O'Keeffe home is next door.

Dressed in Adobe architecture, proper for northern New Mexico, the Inn and Museum are not on the way to anywhere. Sixty miles west of Taos. One hundred miles north of Albuquerque.

Georgia liked her privacy. She was born in 1887 and lived until 1986.

Ms. O'Keeffe was considered a modernist artist. Perhaps, most well-known for painting large flowers and the lands of New Mexico. She was trained in New York in the early 1900's. O'Keeffe was also involved in a bit of a scandal when she allowed photographer Alfred Stiegliz, who she later married to take and publish "sensuous" photos of herself.

After her husband's death, she moved permanently to New Mexico, where she had been visiting to paint for many years. O'Keeffe has been quoted in saying, "It is as if in my one life I have lived many lives."

Though I have never posed nude, I know the feeling.

Sleep came early. The bed was by far the most comfortable on the ride. Georgia would have been proud. Dinner was simple food at the gas station down the road, which has a cafe.

Breakfast the next day came late. Then I mounted up to ride. I pressed the start button. Crank, crank, crank, but no start.

I smelled gas. I had left the fuel valve on all night.

Marilyn drank too much last night. It's my fault really. But we are both paying the price for the hangover. Marilyn was doing fuel shooters into the oil all night long.

I am briefly annoyed, then I remembered, I am in no rush. I walked to the front desk, "Can I have the room one more night?"

"With pleasure, sir."

The google search goes something like, "DR650 non-start, smell gas." Ten or twelve posts in I read to remove the oil fill cap and check for the smell of fuel.

I walked to the bike. Yep, appears to be gas in the oil.

I walked back to the room.

The consensus is to change the oil and turn off the fuel valve (petcock) when not riding. I mistakenly assumed the large gas tank causes too much pressure into the carb. Today, I know the float bowl needing adjusting. At the time, I was doing what I knew, and I didn't know much.

Six months later, after the trip and wanting to try a different motorcycle, I sold what I thought was a near perfect motorcycle to a man who's name I do not remember, telling him make sure you keep the fuel valve turned off when not riding. I'm sure he discovered the real issue. I'm sorry man. I would have told you if I had known. Here's hoping an after the fact, unknown to him apology appeases the karma gods.

Back to the bike. I park it in the shade and work out a course of action. The solution presented itself. Walk to the gas station down the road, buy some oil and something to drain the existing oil into and got on with it.

If one needs to do an oil change there is likely not a prettier place than under the trees behind the outdoor dining area at the Abiquiu Inn.

Word to the wise. Never intoxicate your girl past the point of necessary performance. They just pass out.

The good news. Evidently gas and oil mixtures don't explode when one hits the starter button.

I spend two days at the Abiquiu Inn, immersing myself in fine food served in even finer surroundings. During this time, all of the waitresses were waiters. None asked about the motorcycle parked within eyesight. None asked what a grey beard with a southern accent was doing here.

It was just as well. My thoughts were on the company I didn't have. The legal discussions I wasn't enjoying. The dark eyes that held secrets I would never learn.

I also felt a tinge of guilt. The unobtainable Arizona lady had not been a relationship, so why the guilt at enjoying dinner with someone else? Maybe someone was trying to tell me something. Since I didn't know who someone was, I chose to ignore the entire thing.

When one is riding throughout the day, navigating, tending to the bikes needs and your own, the mind is focused. Moving forward becomes the purpose. Small and large vibrations resonate from the ground, through the foot pegs into the handlebars and even the seat.

At night the vibrations come from a different sort of resonance.

Fate may play a hand. Hot Springs and fortunate timing, like horse riding lessons resonate completely, every bit and more so as compelling as blue skies and back road, two wheeled bliss.

"Can I refill your water, sir?" the waiter suddenly appeared.

"Yes, thanks. Since I'm not traveling anywhere tonight, can I see your wine menu?"

"My pleasure." He pivoted, disappeared and in a moment, reappeared, handing me the list.

I scanned the choices, noticing the prices.

Me, "Georgia O'Keeffe must have been fairly well off."

The waiter, "We made some adjustments to the wine list recently, but may I recommend something we still have on hand from the old list?" This chap caught on quick.

Me, "Sure."

Him, "We always hear excellent remarks for the Napa Valley Pinot Grigio."

I spot it at the bottom of the list, well hidden. The price fits the budget, "Sounds great."

I drank it sitting on a bench in the company of low voltage landscape lighting. Soft hues illuminated the cottonwood trees, while I made notes of the days ride.

My notes that evening read like a Nicholas Sparks paragraph. I was uncertain of how all of this would end. I rode knowing that one day I would be looking back at this place. I will have changed. This place will have changed, but my memory will keep it the same. Which will be real? My memory or the changed place?

In one of his books about young love, tragic health, and marriage, Sparks leaves the reader hanging about the fate of his severely ill wife, whom he had married while they were young and while she was ill.

One of the ending sentences pronounces that now, he is old but still wears the wedding band. He has not taken it off, he never had a reason to.

My notes are complete. I realize that I will still be wearing this memory when I am older. I return to the room and open the computer yet again and read.

The year was 1861.

Southwest from this hotel room, at the time was the Arizona Territory, making up what is today western New Mexico and Arizona.

On January 27th, a band of Apache raided a ranch owned by John Ward. Livestock was stolen, and more egregiously, Ward's stepson, a 12-year-old boy, was kidnapped. The boy had but one eye. It is rumored that one of his captor also had just one eye. He was small for his age, looking much younger. Between the eye and his youthful look, he was spared and taken to live with the Apache.

Ward rushed to Lt. Col. Morrison, the commander of Fort Buchanan. Morrison appointed a recent West Point graduate, Lt. George Bascom to round up the offending band of Indians.

Bascom would die a year later in battle in Val Verde, New Mexico Territory, but not before playing a fool headed role in one of the deadliest misplaced assumptions of the entire Indian-Military relations.

Because the raiding band departed riding east, the military assumed they were a part of the Chiricahua Apache. Only too late did they learn that the Coyotero Apache had carried out the raid and the kidnapping, not the Chiricahua.

A party of 54 soldiers made the ride to Apache Pass, where the Chiricahua were known to be. Bascom was certain, as were his superiors, that one of the leaders, a man called Cochise was responsible for the raid and the kidnapping. An erroneous belief but an easy one to make. Cochise had been wrecking violent havoc for years.

Word was sent to Cochise that the military wished to meet with him, purely to talk. Cochise was suspicious but agreed to the meeting, where he was taken prisoner and told his release was dependent on the release of the boy. He rightly told them his people did not have the boy. In a further offense, Bascom ordered Cochise's family also taken prisoner an attempt to further persuade Cochise to have his people release the boy. Cochise, indeed, had not taken the boy.

Cochise escaped and two days later he and a band attacked a group of American and Mexican teamsters, killing and torturing nine Mexicans. He took three Americans hostages, trying to barter them for the release of his family. The military refused, whereupon Cochise fled to Mexico, killing the Americans, leaving their bodies in his wake, knowing the military would soon find the remains.

As a retaliation, the military hung Cochise's brother and nephews.

This began the period known as the Apache Wars.

The kidnapped boy had been born Felix Martinez. His parents were Jesusa Martinez and Santiago Tellez. Jesusa was thought to be Irish. Tellez was Mexican. After Santiago died, Jesusa married the rancher, John Ward.

In a timeline that has been lost to history, Felix was later found, by one of his step brothers, living with the Coyotero Apache. It is possible he spent ten years with the Apache. He had learned their language and their ways.

Eleven years after being kidnapped, he enlisted as a scout for the U.S. Military where he played a role in the last efforts to capture Geronimo and finally end the Apache Wars.

During his time with the military, he was not known as Felix Martinez. Instead, he was called Mickey Free.

One source credit the soldiers for his new name, after a servant in a book by Charles Lever. There were other Apache who went on to become scouts but none had a name as memorable. History is most often written by the victors, and the name Mickey Free was sure to resonate.

Mickey Free inadvertently helped began the Apache Wars and inadvertently played a part in ending them.

Felix Martinez, aka Mikey Free, part Irish, part Mexican, raised Apache, died in 1915 where he had been living, on the reservation of the White Mountain Apache, even though he was not Apache.

He had been a kidnap victim, a military scout, an Indian reservation policeman, a father, four times a husband, and one of the most thought-provoking characters of his day.

Day 15

Abiquiu, Nm to Grants, Nm

Today the pedal bikers multiply and I learn that God's definition of green is a different shade of dirt.

It's difficult to grow grass in Grants, NM.

Judging from the last hundred miles of sand I slid through today, it's difficult to grow anything, anywhere near Grants. Holy mother of moon craters. This New Mexico portion of this ride is humbling.

I have no notes of my ride from Abiquiu, New Mexico to Grants, New Mexico. But I do remember the sand. Miles and miles of sand. There was no escaping it.

I do have a few photographs. As I view them, I remember taking them. All three photos were taken towards the end of the day. I can make an easy assumption for this. The Abiquiu Inn is a difficult place to leave. Knowing me, I arose late, enjoyed a late breakfast served by a polite, well-trained waiter. I likely ate an omelet with orange juice and about fifteen cups of java.

I do remember the first section of the day's ride being through forest, then those trees gave way to desert. The desert continued into Grants. Once in Grants I discover a resident who has a sense of humor. The sign above the entrance to his driveway reads, "God's Green Acres".

After reaching Grants, NM. near dark, happiness is warm water. Thankfully, Super 8 has lots.

They guy with the yard art could use a little.

The sign among all that brown dirt reads "keep off the grass."

An unremembered day deserves an unmemorable hotel room, which was easily found in Grants. My ride this sunny forested then desert dry day was maybe five and a half hours. It is a five-and-a-half-hour blur.

Grants lies along the now historic and substantially less traveled Route 66. Grants is also an exit from East to West running, Interstate 40, so it receives a fair amount of, "I need gas" or "it's time for a hotel" stop; hence the ease of finding an unmemorable hotel room.

Unmemorable rooms have unmemorable Wi-Fi and this room was no exception. Pulling out my hair and whining did not improve the speed.

The year was 1829.

A boy child was born to Apache parents, members of the Bendonkohe Band. The child was one of eight children, though the other seven would not grow to become a legend.

He was born at the southwest reaches of the final falling altitude of the Continental Divide in the United States, along the Upper Gila River in middle Arizona, to the west of this hotel.

His father died when the boy was young. The boy's grandfather, Mahko, lived on. Mahko was a chief. The boy would never become a chief. He would become much more.

He married for the first time at the age of seventeen. During his long life he was to marry eight more times.

Near the end of his long, brutal and bold life, he was used as a political prop, appearing in the inauguration of President Theodore Roosevelt, riding on horseback down Pennsylvania Avenue in full headdress and war paint. But that was after all of the killing.

The boy grew up during the most severely violent period of Indian-American relations. The relations between Indians and Mexicans were, if possible, even worse. Kidnappings, torture, slaughter, and distrust were woven into the boy's noetic path to adulthood. Once a man, he saw more of the same.

Time was far removed from the days of one cabin being built on native lands. The cabins had multiplied, bringing an Army with them. There was no great grandson capable in numbers or in armament capable of driving the intruders away.

Not only could they not be driven away, they were now doing the driving, sending natives onto smaller and smaller pieces of land, much of it void of game, fish, even water. Most complied. It was that or die.

A few did not. This boy would not.

During his life he witnessed the killing of women and children by Mexican soldiers and came to hate them with a vengeance which would see him lead or participate in revenge raids throughout Arizona, New Mexico, and Mexico. He and his braves matched tit for tat the beheadings, torture, dismemberments, disembowelments of the Mexican Army. At first, he did not hold the same hatred towards the American soldiers. This would later change.

Over a thirty-five-year period, beginning when he was twenty years old, he led exodus after exodus from the reservation. He also would lead at least three different bands of Apache in raids against Mexicans, Americans, the Mexican military, and the American military.

Such were the exploits of the child become legend that not only did he elude capture, but when he finally did surrender in 1885, the United States military refused to have him hung, even though the citizens demanded it. But, instead, he was treated as a military prisoner of war and sent to a reservation where he lived the final twenty-three years of his life. At one point, twenty five percent of the Army was chasing him.

His list of resistance and revenge includes breakouts from three reservations; fighting in the Robledo Mountains; fighting in the Sierra Madre Mountains; plundering along the Sonora River to replenish his weapons and ammunition; attacking wagon trains, ranches; and retreating into the mountains and into Mexico to regroup, then attacking again.

Upon his surrender, the boy who had been born into a time of murder both in war and in revenge, had reached the age of fifty-six.

Though not his real name, the boy known as Geronimo died at the age of 80, on a reservation, in

Florida, where he had been sent after his surrender. He did not prevail, but he fought. His name lives on.

Day 16 and 17

Grants, Nm to Pie Town, Nm

Today, I eat pie!

The Continental Divide ride arrives in Pie Town, New Mexico by way of cow. Even though the land north of Pie Town is sparsely grassed, there are cows. Where there are cows there must also be water. Most of the water that I saw during the day was in large circular troughs.

A peddle biker I met during the day advised that he carried a map showing which of these troughs he could use to fill his jug. Not all ranch owners desire to have riders walking their land and using their water. The trough water still needed purification and the peddler was prepared.

Before riding through cow country, the route departs Grants, New Mexico, goes south, first under Interstate 40, then traversing Zuni Canyon Road, running through a large wash, then past Chute Mesa, past Quartz Hill Trailhead, until it becomes known as Forest Service Road 50.

The section after passing under Interstate 40 is one sandy mess. I walked a portion for fear of burning out the clutch. Pushing Marilyn through sand for fifty yards was about as much fun as wresting a pig on a summer day in the south.

Not that I've ever done such a thing.

Soon, Forest Service Road 50 dead ends and the route turns left onto Ice Caves Road, a paved section of about a mile until my GPS shows a right turn into Cibola County 42.

Vegetation is sparce, a greenish brown, unsure of its ability to grow in such dry, sandy soil. This is not the New Mexico of the Madison Avenue Marketers hired to bring tourists to the state.

An overhead view reveals mostly brown with dots of green. The chamber of commerce focuses their attention on northern New Mexico, an entirely different photo op. Northern towns like Taos draw tourist like a Californian legislator to a new tax.

I ride on, knowing pie is my reward for enduring a trail of dust. The route bisects two areas of greater structure, dark brown though they be. To the west lies Chain of Craters Wilderness Study Area. To the east lies El Malpais National Monument, which gets its name from the Spanish word malpais, loosely meaning "badlands". Well named. The area is covered in volcanic rubble.

The area is so remote and forsaken that it was considered by the Manhattan Project as a candidate for early atomic bomb detonations.

To the west Chain of Craters is a collection of cones where lava rose through the earth's crust. The entire section of the ride has a beauty different from mountain peaks and high-altitude lakes. This geography is akin the skin of an alligator. A sandy alligator.

Before reaching all of this cragged land the route passed to the east of the Ramah Navajo Reservation. I had read of this place the morning of setting off for this section.

This reservation makes up less than one percent in land mass of total Navajo lands, and has a population of about two-thousand.

It is believed that the Ramah Navajo sided with the Zuni in defending territory from Spanish gold seeker Coronado.

As the day progresses, Marilyn grows dusty, caked on like a sticky film. I wonder what this endless dust attack is doing to her fork seals. Actually, I know what it is doing. I just choose to ignore it.

I pass the TLC Ranch and meet another peddler. He tells me that he has been looking forward to reaching Pie Town since leaving the Canadian Border.

He talks of a free hostel in Pie Town, with a fence lined with old toasters, the hostel owned by a kind lady who is often not at home but always leaves the door unlocked. Later I would view the toasters firsthand, all lined up in the New Mexican landscape, some sideways, some upright, all having toasted their last slice of bread years ago.

Next, I pass the Dreamcatcher Ranch, which is purported to have an airstrip. I envision the ranch owner flying friends and relatives onto the property then to all hop in a truck and hit Pie Town for a blackberry Cobbler.

I bid the peddler goodbye, wishing him warm pie and a toaster evening. Very soon, I ride dead end onto Highway 60 and turn left for the half mile ride to the Pie Town Ohana Café.

According to New Mexico dot org, Pie town got its name from a bakery which opened there by Clyde Norman in the early 1920's. Population is two hundred, more or less, depending on who you ask, which census year is to be believed and whether the annual pie festival is in full force.

Pie Town is remote. One needs to be riding through to stumble upon it. Or walking through or peddling through.

As Forest Gump's friend famously almost said, "You got your apple pie, your blackberry pie, your strawberry pie, your raspberry pie, your thick crust pie, your thin crust pie, your cobbler pie, your double crust pie..."

None of which should be confused with your pot pie, chiffon pie, meringue pie, shepherd's pie, custard pie, tart pie, or your ice cream pie.

All in all, there are four pie establishments in pie town and lordy, lordy, of all amazing the facts about Pie Town, they have a real estate office. The lady working at the pie establishment where I ordered an apple pie with vanilla ice cream was as lovely as the pie, without any of the crust. She was also a realtor, and a singer, as I would find out the next day.

The ride from Grants to Pie Town was fairly easy, one might say almost as easy as pie. Except, I've never had sand in my pie. The sand was tiring. The pie and the realtor, singer, pie baker was not tiring. As I sat and enjoyed all of this blood sugar raising deliciousness, I made a decision. I would stay for a day or so. There were more flavors to try. I asked the pie lady if there was a hotel nearby.

"Yep, just down the road in Datil."

Me, "Thanks, the pie was great."

"You should hang around a couple of days. There is a western show tomorrow. Let me get you a flyer." She hands me a printout with directions.

"Thanks, I might do that."

"Come see it. I promise the musical entertainment will be worth the visit."

Just down the road turns out to be twenty-one miles.

I spent two nights at the hotel in Datil. The western event was a blast and yes, the music was a treat. The pie lady sang as her husband sang and accompanied on guitar. They performed an array of old western standards. A vendor had been set up. More pie was consumed.

The entire event was staged in a "Western Town" recreated by a man intent on creating his own piece of history. Located in the Town of Gabriella, 20 miles from Datil, and forty-eight miles from Pie Town, the place has twenty wooden buildings, painted green, red and grey, an old stage coach, and two horse drawn carriages.

Encompassing twenty-eight acres, the town has a bath house, hotel, saloon and power supplied by a generator.

What to do if you have a soft spot for old western towns, with a saloon, livery and marshal's office? If you are Larry Iams, and you happen to own a large plot of land in extremely rural New Mexico, you build yourself such a town. You name it Gabriella. Then you throw a big party.

As I walk among the buildings, I half expect Cochise to come riding out of the brush and the burn the place to the ground. More likely a realtor will arrive in a four-wheel drive Chevy and hand me a business card.

The best news is that as of 2022 the town is for sale, so what are you waiting for pilgrim? Saddle up and make your home at #250 Frontier Trail. I did. At least for a few hours.

After good music, good pie and a good deal of western attire, I fire up Marilyn and ride back to the hotel in Datil. Its late afternoon. I find food down the road in Pie Town and return to the room. Tomorrow I will continue. Maybe.

Marilyn took it all in. On the ride back to the hotel, she backfired. Twice. What to make of this gesture? Your guess is as good as mine.

Recovering from a nap induced by too much food, the wi-fi is fired to life.

The year was 1858.

Mexican Colonel Carrasco was leading a mission of four hundred soldiers. For many years the Mexican military had been unsuccessful in reining in the attacks on locals by Apache. In his mind, the only good Apache was either a reservation living Apache or a dead Apache. From the Apache perspective the feeling was mutual and they considered the Mexican military not to be trusted.

The Apache had rightly earned a reputation of vile killing. So had the Mexican military. History will judge the justification for the killing. Colonel Carrasco was not interested in historical judgement. He wanted the Apache raids to end. There was enough distrust on both sides to build a long bridge of hatred.

Colonel Corrasco was about to add to the distrust. He offered his troops one-hundred pesos for a male Apache scalp and fifty pesos for a woman or child's scalp. The men obliged.

When Geronimo learned of the slaughter he joined two other bands, one led by Cochise. They set out for Arizpe, a Mexican garrison. When fighting was done, few Mexicans survived. Geronimo was never a chief, but his name will forever be held in high esteem by his people.

The fighting, for Geronimo, would continue for fifteen more years. He led raid after raid, after which retreating to hide often in Mexico.

I turn off the computer and bring myself back to the world of today. I touch my hair. Thankfully it is still on my head.

Back to fine baristas and long days on the motorcycle. I scan through the photos on my phone.

Memories line up like dominoes. Touch them too forcefully and they topple into the past.

White steam smoke from the train in Chama, the rocky, muscular, climb north of Butte, Montana. The demanding figures that are the Tetons. And more. Each already growing into the unconscious background that is the canvas upon which this motorcycle has painted north to south.

I am ready to be done. But I don't wish it to be over. The remote back roads of this country, when ridden solo, are as endearing as they are precipitous.

Some of them are rocky. Others smooth and easy. A few will take you to views otherwise unseen. And one, at least, will lead you to pie. Make mine apple.

Yesterday, a roadside curiosity, and a hankering for a Cliff bar, lure me to stop. The sign says, "Ice cave" ok, I'll bite.

Eighty-seven downward stairs later, the temp drops from 80 to 35. Nice place to nibble that Cliff bar. White chocolate macadamia nut, since you asked.

The landscape leaving the ice caves had Marilyn playing wagon train damsel to Clint's high plains drifter. Easy on the eyes, but road worn and enough already of the desert wind.

With any rain the way these grassy plains roads would be as wide and unforgiving as your aunt Maybell's temper.

But once Maybell calms down, she bakes one heck of a pie.

On the property of the Ice Cave there was an old gas pump, rusting away.

The memories line up. Some more tasty than others.

Day 18

Datil, Nm to Silver City, Nm

Today, I discover blue hair and yoga.

The Beatles likely didn't have southern New Mexico in mind when they sang of the long and winding road. If they had, one of the boys would have surely inserted lonely between long and winding.

One hundred thirty miles to the north, departing Datil, a Netleaf Hackberry draws one's eye towards the endless western horizon, where settlers once focused their hopes. Mules hitched. Wheels turning.

Long and winding and lonely.

As the bike takes me nearer Silver City, the land changes becoming more appealing.

Yucca have made an appearance. One particularly fine example, standing along the dust and brush, welcomes me to Silver City, New Mexico, in the foothills of the Pinos Altos mountains.

Working my way around and through Silver City I see a coffee shop. Yippie yi yaeee.

The place has comfy chairs. The barista has blue hair. I have a blue jacket, so we match. Her hair has a red streak on the left side.

My jacket didn't have a red streak dyed in on one side, and didn't need one. Her hair didn't need one either, but somehow it worked.

"What can I get started for you?"

I think to myself but don't say, "here we go again."

The menu on the wall behind her was not a black chalk board. It was a green chalk board. With white handwritten sandwiches for sale. One caught my eye.

'Hand Karved Karma Turkey'

I considered this. "Did anyone ask the turkey?" I don't say it aloud but want to.

Another item 'Chakra Chicken and Pine Nuts'

Then I see it. "Yoga man Yogurt with Berries."

"I'll have the yogurt and a large coffee."

Her, "Good choice."

Me, thinking but not saying, "here we go again."

She wore a long flowing bright red toga thing. It swirled as she spun away.

I've never tried yoga, but the yogurt was well balanced.

The day was winding down. I was winding down. Marilyn, parked outside was leaning down. She always leaned left, but I tried not to hold it against her.

A relatively simple machine, as machines go, she had carried me two thousand miles. She had climbed high rocky paths, swooped through winding gravel laden back country, dodged hail and high winds and through it all had only gotten drunk once. All this while following a long blue line. A line I had drawn back in Ridgway, Colorado.

If she kept going, I had but one more day on the blue line.

I rise for a refill.

Barista, "Anyone ever tell you the outfit looks like a smurf?"

I do a little sidestep, complete with head nod in same direction, then in slow motion, point one finger to my head, and then towards her locks.

"You are funny." Says she.

"I get that a lot." Says I.

"Either I need your jacket, or you need my hair."

I take off the jacket, holding it outward, almost hoping she takes it. It's nearly worn out. I bought it used and have used it well over the last few years. If I replace it with a black one, I won't hear Smurf jokes.

Her "I can't do that to you. What else would you ever find to match those pants?"

Me. "Well, Dang."

I find an old hotel in town and see another DR650 parked in front, so I park next to it. There is also another motorcycle parked there. I was to learn, later, that they belonged to a couple who had ridden from Arizona, enjoying the Summer and the fine roads between Arizona and Silver City.

The hotel room was small in size. I didn't care. I had all I needed. A bed. A bath and internet.

The year was 1874.

Just down the street from this hotel, a mother and father, Mr. and Mrs. Antrim, lived with their two sons. The mother was named Catherine and was of poor health, suffering from tuberculosis. The father, worked as a miner, drank and gambled and often was not at home. The family had moved west in a failed attempt to assist the mother's health.

She died, in 1874, a year after moving to Silver City. Her sons were close to her and took it very hard.

The father left the boys in the care of two different families in Silver City and he left for Arizona. One of his sons began to get into trouble, first stealing clothes, being jailed, escaping and heading out into the world on his own at the tender age of fifteen.

In the same year, across the country, in Texas, a young man was hunting buffalo. His name was Patrick. Patrick had no way of knowing that he was to be involved with one of Silver City's most notorious alumni.

Patrick, like the fifteen-year-old in Silver City, had suffered tremendous loss.

Patrick had been born in Chambers County Alabama, to John and Elizabeth.

His parents had immigrated from England and when Patrick was three. His father, looking to make the family's fortunes in agriculture, purchased a plantation in Louisiana. Poor historical timing ended this dream. The Civil War crushed the enterprise. Then, Patrick's mother died at the age of thirty-seven. One year later his father John died at the age forty-five, leaving the family in debt.

Young Patrick, now 18, headed west. First a buffalo hunter, then a cowboy in New Mexico. He married, only to have his wife die two weeks later. After living this amount of heartache, many would have given up. Patrick did not.

In 1880 he married again and in November of 1880, at the age of twenty-nine, was elected Sheriff of Lincoln County New Mexico.

The west was as wild as the buffalo he once hunted and men filled with all manner of criminal indignation roamed throughout. One of these men was the abandoned child in Silver City, now grown.

The son of Mr. and Mrs. Antrim was wanted for murder in New Mexico and had eluded capture often by crossing territory lines.

After Silver City, he went on to work at a ranch where he got into an altercation with a blacksmith, who is reported to have been drinking at a saloon owned by George Adkins, in Camp Grant, Arizona. Catherine's loving son shot and killed the blacksmith.

He rode back to New Mexico and worked at a ranch but soon turned to rustling cattle with a man named Tunstall, of whom he was fond, a second father figure.

Tunstall would later be killed by men who had been deputized to find him. It was said that the men could have brought in Tunstall, but instead killed him, unarmed. Upon hearing the news, Catherine's son swore revenge. He and others found the men and when they tried to run, he shot them both dead.

But he figured the job as only half done. He wanted the Sheriff who had deputized the men and set a trap for the Sheriff, Brady. Soon enough Brady had been killed.

Whether Sheriff Brady asked the deputized men to kill Tunstall, whether the men did it on their own, whether Tunstall was unarmed, all of this will be forever unknown.

What is known is that the boy from Alabama, Patrick, now thirty years old, knew the fugitive had killed several men, one of whom was a Sheriff, and he was going to bring him in. And he did.

Patrick obtained a deputy U.S. Marshall commission in order to track the fugitive across government lines.

In 1881, Patrick, known as Pat, last name Garrett, and a posse, lie in wait at Fort Sumner, New Mexico. They had information that Catherine's son, would be there. The son, born as William Henry McCarty Antrim, aka, William Bonney, aka Billy the Kid.

A gun fight ensued. One of Billy's compadres was killed. Billy escaped.

Three days later, Patrick Garrett got his man in a place called Stinking Springs, killing another of Billy's gang in the melee and capturing Billy.

The Kid was sentenced to hang, but The Kid escaped, killing two guards in the process.

The boy who lost both parents by the time he was eighteen and a wife by the time he was twenty-two, mounted up and rode. He knew of a likely friend of the Kid. Sure enough, the Kid was found.

Sheriff Garrett waited in the house, standing, he would later say, in the shadows. Billy the Kid called out, "who is there?" The answer came in the form of two-gun shots, one hitting Billy near the heart.

Sheriff Garrett, would live only twenty-seven more years, murdered in 1908. A special coffin had to be built. He was six feet five inches tall.

His grave is in the Masonic Cemetery, Las Cruces, New Mexico.

Billy the Kid is buried in Fort Sumner. Today, in a warped sense of priority, his grave is surrounded by a metal cage to prevent souvenir hunters.

No medal of honor lies on the grave of Pat Garret, but should.

Day 19

Silver City, Nm, to the US/Mexico Border

Today I achieve a goal. And discover that some goals are beyond my ability to comprehend.

It's less than two hundred miles from Silver City to the border of Mexico. Two hundred miles after riding two thousand is not a burden. I am content. The weather is content. Marilyn is content. We ride on pavement most of the day.

Roadside images fly by, sage and brown grass. They guide me towards my goal, lining the road with open arms, scraggly though they be. I am near the border. There is no one, anywhere. Then I pass a border patrol truck coming from the opposite direction. They wave. I wave back, suspecting they have seen more than their share of motorcyclist, peddlers and hikers on this road.

I press the bike to the speed limit. I can feel it. Within twenty-five miles now. What would the border look like? Would there be an official looking building? I ride on.

Then I see him.

Twenty miles from reaching the Mexican border I spot a man walking. In the opposite direction. Towards me. Surely, he can't be just beginning the trail to Canada. The approaching winter won't allow such a hike.

I decide to ride on, turn around at the border and approach him with an offer of my remaining Gatorade. It is eighty-five degrees. He is carrying a gallon milk jug, partially filled with water.

I reach the border and take the necessary photo. Then, I turn around. I ride twenty miles back. He is still there. Walking. This is how I meet Daniel.

Daniel has been walking for a while.

Three years to be exact. Daniel had walked across America. Walked. No motorcycle. No bicycle. Not even a skateboard.

He had walked the Appalachian trial, then Pacific crest trail, and yesterday had completed the Continental Divide trail.

First Ethan in Jackson, Wyoming. Now Daniel. How many more are out there?

At 3:30 in the hot afternoon, Daniel, on this day had walked twenty-two miles. Tonight, he will sleep on the side of the road, out of eyesight of the road, but nearby. The border patrol know he is there. They have given him water. Tonight, will be his third night on this road.

We spoke for about fifteen minutes. He was well read, well intentioned, humorous, proud, but not boastful of his accomplishment and clear eyed.

We compared notes of our overlapping journey. Sights seen. Towns visited. Desert sand endured. Daniel had seen many of the same sights, only more closely. I spun two wheels. He lifted two feet. I will be in a hotel tonight. He will sleep on a mat in the desert, under a small tarp.

One may think he, like Ethan are searching for something they will never find. Maybe. Maybe they just want to DO something. I understand.

Today, I achieved a goal. I completed the Continental Divide Ride.

I was proud, happy, content, even a bit astonished.

Hubris had but twenty miles, to shine its false light.

Then, I had met Daniel. I was reluctant to leave him there in the sun. He assured me that not only was he fine, but that he planned to walk to Alaska by next Summer.

Thirty miles to the north, after meeting Daniel, I stop to photograph an abandoned church. It seemed fitting. For reason or reasons, I will not presume to know. Some goals are beyond my comprehension.

I have nothing now to do but to sit atop this machine and ride easy pavement miles back to Montrose, Colorado, pick up the truck and camper and find a good coffee shop, with a chalkboard menu.

There, I would make a new plan.

I figured my ride was over, that there would be no more moments of wonder, large or small. I did not know that the grandeur of the twelve-thousand-foot Rocky Mountains was about to be matched by a mere three inches.

After making my way back to Silver City, I remember a road recommended by Nate Bon and Halley

Baggins, the two motorcycle riders who I met in Silver City. They spoke of Highway 180 into Alpine, AZ, a road full of sweeping curves. Some roads are made for motorcycles. This is one of them.

While riding Highway 180, my eyes begin to see things.

The road begins to crawl. In three decades of riding motorcycles, I've never seen a road crawl. My chin went dead center, held slightly higher, eyes squinted.

What the hell?

The crawl began to form a pattern. Then detail emerged. Detail in the form of one little creature at a time. Crawling across the pavement. Thousands of them. With a singular goal. Working their way west. Intent to make a destination somewhere out of sight. Evidently goals aren't just a human condition.

What they are, I haven't a clue. Perhaps they had a map. Perhaps one of their kind had created a route. Maybe they were on the final leg of a trifecta.

I paused for a photo and wished them well.

May their adventure be as rewarding as my Great Continental Divide Ride.

Epilogue

Once back in Colorado, I speak to a dear friend, someone I trusted in these matters; and mentioned my feelings for Samantha. I expected her to say, "are you crazy?" Instead, I heard, "You have to tell her."

So, I packed up the camper and drove to Arizona. And one night at a restaurant named Desert Rose, I told her.

It was one of the most potentially embarrassing moments of my life. I knew the reply would be, if not laughter, a polite no.

I was wrong. The reply was a huge smile. Go figure.

The year was 2016.

Samantha and I are living in Northern Phoenix. She trains horses. I train my fingers to do a poor but acceptable imitation of Stevie Ray Vaughn's "Mary had a Little Lamb".

I know how I'd like our relationship to proceed. I know the word I would like to use when introducing her.

There is a something I would like to ask her.

I have done this before. This, being asking an important question. My previous experience was not handled poorly exactly, it was just not asked well. The asking had more to do with my needs than the lady on the other end of the question.

This time I would like to do better.

But I had no plan. This wore on me. Time was not on my side. A certain date was coming up. I needed a plan and I did not know where to find it.

It was likely that Samantha would be on this earth thirty years longer than I.

If I could give her a memory that would endure three decades, only then would I have done well.

One afternoon, watching Sam ride a young horse in a round pen, I saddled up Sam's mare, named Bella. I had learned to ride on Bella. Bella was well trained. She accepted my short comings. Once tacked up, I put foot in stirrup, hoisted upwards and settled in.

I nudged Bella into the arena.

I look to my left and see Sam leaving the round pen. She sits easily in the saddle and walks her horse towards the barn. The horse was young, the new kid at the place.

As Sam rode, the land inclined, until it became a small knoll. Sam always directed horses around this feature. Today, she rode directly onto it.

Once atop, she stopped and waved at me, her arm, high in the air.

A lone rider against the sky.

My heart stopped. My breath caught up short. At that very instant I knew. The image was one I had seen before, not in real life but I had seen it, and now I had a plan.

One week later.

The moon was full. The Arizona evening air was brilliant, dry, calm, seventy degrees with pristine expectation.

Today was Sam's birthday.

The last horsc had been fed. Tack had been put away. The barn had been closed down. Water for each stall had been filled. Lights had been turned off.

"Come ride with me." I say.

"What?"

"Come ride with me, just you and I. In the arena. Let's take Bella and the new kid."

She hesitated. I could see her thinking. Its dark, horses don't see that well in the dark. We had just put everything up.

I say, "You and me. Bareback. A walk around the arena."

Sam, "You know it's dark, right?"

I take her hand say once more, "Come ride with me."

We walk to the stalls. Sam gathers Bella and the new kid and has them ready in less than five minutes.

We walk them through the gate. Each of us, in turn make use of a mounting block, grab a handful of mane and climb aboard. Me on Bella, her on the new kid.

Sam looks at me, I give away nothing. We walk the horses into the center of the arena. Moonlight catches Sam and I am taken by emotion. Hold it together boy. Don't mess this up.

I bring Bella to a stop. Sam brings the new kid to a stop. With my left heel I nudge Bella. Her training kicks in and she side passes, closer to Sam.

I look at Sam. She looks at me, head slightly askew, a questioning expression on her face.

This has to endure thirty years. For a moment, I second guess myself. Then, I decide to put my trust in a dream.

I begin, "Sam, I met you on a horse,"

I continue, "I came to know you on a horse." Her gaze intensifies.

"I fell in love with you on a horse." I pause again. I see tears welling up in her eyes.

"It's only fitting that I ask you to marry me on a horse. Will you marry me, Sam?"

The year is 2022.

Sam still trains horses, riding to client's properties on her Suzuki Vstrom 650. I pilot two old Harleys. Bella is retired. The new kid has moved on to a happy owner. I still play music.

I still carry Sam's card in my wallet. I have never removed Sam's card from my wallet. I have never had a reason to.

Credits and Sources

1. Coffee Why? Because it is the world's most widely used drug.

   Two billion cups a day are consumed worldwide. Two billion. Second only to water and tea.

   Believed to have originated in Ethiopia, coffee made it way throughout Persia in the 15th century.

   There are stories of goat herders noticing their enlivened goats after eating coffee beans.

   There are stories of Monks then using the beans to make a drink.

   Whatever its origins, coffee had arrived.

   The age of enlightenment followed. Of course, it did. Mathematics evolved. Machines were invented. People were focused.

   An early Monk was overheard asking the age-old question. "What is a Starbucks? And how many will fit on the head of a pin?"

By the 17th century Coffee was widely used in Europe. Like drugs everywhere it was condemned by many religious leaders until the Pope himself granted approval.

Many people at the time drank more alcohol than water, due to the disease spread by unsanitary water. Coffee, being boiled, was safe and soon replaced alcohol as a morning beverage.

Employers everywhere rejoiced.

By 1625, Johann Sebastian Bach was so enamored by coffee he wrote a cantata about the beverage.

In 1845 Henry David Thoreau made his way to Walden Pond where he attempted to live simply. While drinking coffee.

Musicians, Writers, Philosophers, Kings, Sailors, Senators, long distance motorcycle riders, Blondes, Brunettes, the Tie Dyed, the Blue hairs, both young and old, all drink coffee.

Sources include:

Live Science

Wikipedia

"The Apache Wars"

Navajo-NSN.gov

Britannica.com

American History.net

United States now.org

Legends of America.com

Utetribe.com

Warpaths2peacepipes.com

Nez Perce.org

FS.USA.gov

Biography.com

History Link.org

History of Colorado Encyclopedia.org

Idahogeneology.com

Discovering Montana.com

National geographic.com

Library of Congress

NewMexico.org

Recommendations

Thank you for reading! If you've enjoyed this edition of Marylyn Across America, check out our other ride diary:

- *Marylyn Across America:*

   ### *The Trans-America Trail*

About the Author

Jeff Fletcher is a musician, author and editor living in Arizona with his wife Samantha.

Having ridden motorcycles on pavement throughout most of the United States and New Zealand, he decided, at age 55, to try off-road long-distance adventure riding.

Relying on the wisdom and maps of those who pioneered such adventures, he rode the Trans-America Trail east to west and the Continental divide, north to south.

This book chronicles the ups, the downs, the scenery and the endless array of enduring personalities he encountered along the way.

It's a big, beautiful country.

Come along for the ride of a lifetime!

Review

<u>Marilyn Across America</u>

on Amazon today!

The author appreciates you taking the time to review this book on Amazon. Here's how to do it:

1.   Go to the detail page for the book by searching "Marilyn Across America Book 2" on Amazon.com (If you've placed an order for the item, you can also go to Your Orders)

2.   Click "Write a Customer Review" in the Customer Reviews section.

3.   Select a Star Rating. If you'd like to leave a written review you can do so below the star rating section.

4.   Click Submit.

Every rating and review helps us reach a wider audience. Thank you for your support!

Made in the USA
Monee, IL
15 February 2023

27836217R00167